江西财经大学优秀青年学术人才支持计划资助

英汉交替传译信息忠实度评估研究

Assessment of Information Fidelity in English-Chinese Consecutive Interpreting

肖　锐　著

浙江工商大学出版社
ZHEJIANG GONGSHANG UNIVERSITY PRESS
· 杭州 ·

图书在版编目(CIP)数据

英汉交替传译信息忠实度评估研究 / 肖锐著. —杭州:浙江工商大学出版社,2023.3

ISBN 978-7-5178-5224-7

Ⅰ.①英… Ⅱ.①肖… Ⅲ.①英语—口译—研究 Ⅳ.①H315.9

中国版本图书馆 CIP 数据核字(2022)第227513号

英汉交替传译信息忠实度评估研究

YINGHAN JIAOTI CHUANYI XINXI ZHONGSHIDU PINGGU YANJIU

肖　锐 著

策划编辑	姚　媛
责任编辑	王　英
责任校对	林莉燕
封面设计	朱嘉怡
责任印制	包建辉
出版发行	浙江工商大学出版社
	(杭州市教工路198号　邮政编码310012)
	(E-mail:zjgsupress@163.com)
	(网址:http://www.zjgsupress.com)
	电话:0571-88904980,88831806(传真)
排　　版	杭州朝曦图文设计有限公司
印　　刷	广东虎彩云印刷有限公司绍兴分公司
开　　本	710mm×1000mm　1/16
印　　张	14
字　　数	212千
版 印 次	2023年3月第1版　2023年3月第1次印刷
书　　号	ISBN 978-7-5178-5224-7
定　　价	56.00元

List of Abbreviations

PA	Propositional Analysis
QI	Quality in Interpreting
CI	Consecutive Interpreting
SI	Simultaneous Interpreting
TPR	Translation Process Research
T & I	Translation and Interpretation
EOI	Error, Omission and Infelicity
EIC	English Interpreting Certificate
TIS	Translation and Interpreting Study
IS	Interpreting Studies
TL	Target Language
SL	Source Language
EA	Error Analysis
SLA	Second Language Acquistion
MTI	Master of Translation and Interpreting
BTI	Bachelor of Translation and Interpreting
TTR	Type-Token Ratio
MFRM	Multi-Faceted Rasch Measurement
RRE	Rater Reliability Estimate
CTT	Classical Test Theory

IRR	Inter-Rater Reliability
PC	Propositional Correspondence
WE	Well-performing Examinee
UE	Under-performing Examinee

Contents

List of Figures

List of Tables

Chapter 1

Introduction

This study, drawing upon theoretical and methodological insights from interpreting studies (IS), semantics, textual analysis and testing theory, is an interdisciplinary investigation into English-Chinese consecutive interpreting (CI) in an attempt to discuss propositional analysis (PA) in the assessment of information fidelity of consecutive interpreting, by means of proposing a theoretical framework and conducting empirical validation. Besides, the present study goes deep into the quest for the application of propositional analysis in interpreter training, through discussions of examinees' problems foregrounded in their performance, and implications of PA for interpreter trainers. To start with, this chapter is to briefly outline the research motivations, significance, questions and blueprint of the whole study.

1.1 Motivations for the Study

1.1.1 Why Study the Assessment of Information Fidelity in Consecutive Interpreting

Assessment of the quality of interpreting, whether in a holistic approach or an analytical approach, falls within three categories: information fidelity, delivery and target language quality (Lee, 2008; Lee, 2015; Han, 2015). Among these three essential components of interpreting quality, information fidelity ranks the top in importance and weight in assessment. With that said, research on quality assessment, especially on information fidelity, which is to be combed through in Chapter 2, has aroused waves of interest among scholars in the field of linguistics, translation and interpreting studies (TIS), and testing.

Despite the enthusiasm thrown in assessment of interpreting fidelity and the bulk of endeavors committed in this realm, both in theoretical and methodological aspects, a rough study of the literature reveals that the concept of information fidelity varies significantly according to groups of audience, settings and criteria. The inherently subjective nature of the assessment of information fidelity lends itself to controversies and criticism over reliability of research outcomes.

Further, lightening-speed development of artificial intelligence and deep learning has made it possible to realize machine-based quality assessment of some components of interpreting assessment: delivery and idiomaticity. Still, the machine-based information fidelity assessment has met its glass ceiling, partially due to lacking of an objective and feasible assessment criterion.

Hence, there are disciplinary and industrial impetuses behind the present investigation to explore the possibility of a fidelity-assessment criterion that is objective and operable. For a holistic approach, information fidelity is entangled with other criteria. There is a tendency of "halo effect" during assessment, namely, judges are likely to be affected by certain aspect(s) of performance (Gile, 1990), making assessment completely prone to subjectivity, especially among non-professionals. Convenient as it is, a holistic approach of this kind is unable to provide specific or componential information as regards interpreting performance, especially to interpreting researchers or instructors, who are anxious to analyze interpreting performance. As for the analytical approach, assessment criterion consists of several essential components, which mitigates the possibility of "halo effect". However, this criterion, featured with weakness in inter-rater consistency, is subject to personal experiences, backgrounds, and profession, etc. In this regard, Yeh (2015) proposes that researchers draw references from recent development of formal linguistics and develop some objective criteria in the assessment of information fidelity. The present investigation, to answer the call, is to offer a much-wanted alternative criterion to this field of study.

An equally important impetus of the investigation is the pedagogical use of study on the assessment of information fidelity. It is widely acknowledged that study on the issue reveals much information about interpreters' use of interpreting strategies, a source of inspiration and reference to interpreter instructors and trainees. In this regard, the present study will offer a way to link performance assessment and interpreter training.

1.1.2 Why Adopt Propositional Analysis for the Assessment of Information Fidelity

Interpreting is "an activity consisting (mainly) in the production of utterances (texts) which are presumed to have a similar meaning or effect as previously existing utterances in another language and culture" (Pöchhacker, 2015: 22). The controversy lies in "similiar meaning or effect". To what degree could interpreters' information be considered "similar" to the original information and how to measure the similiarity? Scholars endeavor to find explanations from various linguistic branches and from different persepctives of meaning constituency. Still, little consensus has been achieved. A hard-won agreement is that meaning equivalence could not be measured literally, but rather, semantic or pragmatic meaning should be taken into account.

Proposition is regarded as a basic unit of meaning representation in semantics, a formal representation of meaning in memory. The meaning of an utterance (text) is assumed to be represented by a list of connected propositions. Propositions consist of word concepts. Word concepts are abstract entries of lexicons, represented by one or more words in the surface structure. (Turner & Greene, 1977) Propositions are idea units, each one representing a single piece of idea/information. From a functional grammar perspective, meaning is realized in hierarchy, from top to bottom, context, semantics, lexico-grammar and phonology. In this sense, propositional representation is realized at semantic level, if not at lexico-grammar level.

In this sense, proposition can also serve as a basic information assessment unit for analyzing interpreting performance. It is assumed that a hierarchy of information assessment system should represent meaning on three levels: information points, semantic structure and discoursal strucutre. (Cai, 2003) Proposition, which is a basic component of information, semantic relations and macro-structure in semantics, could meet such demands. Such a standard information assessment unit has the potential to mitigate subjectivity in interpreting assessment (cf. Yeh, 2015).

With respect to the theoretical considerations of proposition, it comes to sense that propositional analysis could play a role in the assessment of information fidelity in interpreting. Further, PA has developed a set of value judgment procedures to evaluate propositional correspondence (PC), which makes it suitable for the task of assessing information fidelity in practice. A few investigations have put PA in practice for interpreting assessment. The present study attempts to advance the validation investigation in this regard, both theoretically and methodologically.

1.2 Significance of the Study

Over the past few decades, TIS has enjoyed significant advances in various dimensions, and "has come to embrace a wide rang of types of intercultural encounter and transfer, interfacing with disciplines... Each (discipline) provides different and valid perspectives on translation" (Hubscher-Davidson & Borodo, 2012: ix). Likewise, interpreting quality assessment has experienced great progress in this interface of disciplines and ensuing paradigmatic shifts. (Xiao & Yu, 2017) This investigation is a step forward in this direction, contributing to this undertaking, theoretically, practically and methodologically.

Research on information quality has engaged assessment tools and criteria as foci. Scholars have taken theoretical and methodological references from related fields of social sciences, such as linguistics, sociology, anthropology, cognitive science and psychology, etc. However, information quality assessment has met bottleneck. At present, quality assessment is frequently questioned in terms of subjectivity and a lack of "standardized and feasible information assessment unit" (Cai, 2007: 42), which calls for more sources of disciplinary reference from other fields and psychometrics, including semantics. The study follows the track of inter-disciplinary study and draws references from semantics in an attempt to shed light on interpreting performance assessment and interpreting studies.

With that said, the present research decides to adopt a propositional analysis approach to the assessment of information fidelity in consecutive interpreting, which theorizes the PA-based criterion in this aspect and validate it in a simulated interpreting test. The study proposes that proposition could serve as a basic information assessment unit and PA could offer a set of standard assessment procedures, which contributes to and advances the development of standardized interpreting information assessment that aims at mitigating rater effects and subjectivity.

In addition, with PA-based categories of propostional correspondence, this study makes an exploratory attempt to figure out propositional correspondence patterns, with which we can possibly find the key towards a right path of analyzing examinees' interpreting performance, especially their performance in terms of message transfer.

From a practical perspective, the study offers a practical and operable instrument for the assessment of information fidelity in consecutive interpreting. The assessment instrument is applicable in various interpreting tests, whether nationwide high-stake certificate accreditation tests or in-class diagnostic or formative tests, which definitely will yield some implications for instructors, trainees, test designers and researchers in related fields. Further, the theoretical framework of propositional analysis paves the way for its application in computer-based assessment. The validation of PA could be a thrust to machine-based assessment, an eye-attracting undertaking, especially in the aspect of information fidelity assessment. PA, offering theoretical and practical inspirations to system design in this regard, could be integrated into the constructs of machine-based interpreting assessment. In addition, collected data and materials could serve as a training set and a test set that are essentially needed in machine learning and AI programming.

From a methodological perspective, this study employs a mixed method. For the validation of the PA-based criterion, quantitative research methods are used to extract and analyze test results, including statistical analysis with the help of SPSS and MFRM analysis. When it comes to discussions of propositional distribution and pedagogical implications, qualitative research methods such as feedbacks and interviews are deployed.

1.3 Research Questions

The primary purpose of the study is to validate the PA-based criterion in the assessment of information fidelity in consecutive interpreting, together with its use in interpreter training. For that purpose, the study will theorize an analytical framework of propositional analysis which incorporates theoretical and methodological references from semantics, translation and interpretation (T & I) studies and testing theory. Hence, the major question of this study relates to justification and validation of propositional analysis in the assessment of information fidelity of English-Chinese consecutive interpreting test. Under this overarching question, there are several specific questions that are also inquired herewithin:

① Is it justifiable to apply PA to the assessment of information fidelity in

English-Chinese CI? Or, is the PA-based criterion justifiable in terms of construct validity?

② How does PA perform in the practical assessment of information fidelity in English-Chinese CI? Or, is the PA-based criterion practically justifiable in terms of criterion validity and rater reliability?

③ What are the advantages and disadvantages of the PA-based criterion used in the assessment of information fidelity in English-Chinese CI, in comparison with the English Interpreting Certificate (EIC) Test criterion?

1.4 Data and Methodology

Data used in the present study are extracted from a database of interpreting test materials: audio recordings of the source and interpreted speeches, rating scores of information fidelity based on a conventional assessment criterion and the PA-based criterion, propositionalized transcripts in alignment with the source text, and propositionalized transcripts tagged with correspondence patterns. Recordings are collected in an English-Chinese consecutive interpreting test, held in four universities. Besides, audio recordings are transcribed and then transcripts are transformed into propositions, so as to be suitable for rating work and tagged by raters with the PA-based criterion.

Methodologically, this study will adopt a mixed research method to carry out the research.

The research first conducts a comprehensive review of literature in the field of interpreting quality assessment where the assessment of information fidelity has already been studied and the latest development in theory and methodology. To this end, published papers, monographs and academic projects on this issue are sought after and combed through to find the niche for the subsequent investigation.

After that, a theoretical and analytical framework will be proposed on the basis of propositional analysis in semantics. The framework is designed to theorize construct validity of the PA-based criterion in the assessment of information fidelity.

The present study draws on a mixed research method combining quantitaive and qualitative research. Quantitatively, raw scores of information fidelity based on the PA-based criterion and the EIC criterion will be analyzed in SPSS for inter-rater reliability (IRR) and correlation coefficiency. Then, the raw scores will be put in FACETS, a software for multi-faceted Rasch analysis, for feasibility indicators of the PA-based criterion. Subsequently, frequencies and ratios of different propositional correspondence categories, extracted from taggings in the database, will be computed for pattern distrution and ensuing discussion of pedagogical implications.

To explore the in-depth motivations and sources underlying prominent problems in interpreting performance, qualitative accounts from questionnaire will be examined. These accounts also provide clues for pedagogical discussions that follow.

1.5 Organization of the Book

The current book consists of seven chapters, starting from broad and generic issues to specific inquiries:

Chapter 1 presents a brief introduction to the motivations underlying this study, potential contributions to the related realms, questions to answer and methodologies that are adopted in the investigation.

Chapter 2, a review of theoretical and methodological studies on interpreting quality as well as its assessment is presented in detail. This chapter combs through a bulk of literature on quality assessment studies from the perspectives of interpreting quality assessment in professional and educational contexts. Critical comments are made to pinpoint the niche of the current invesigation.

Chapter 3 associates the assessment of information fidelity with the theory of proposition in semantics, exploring the potential use of PA in interpreting assessment. An analytical framework of the PA-based information fidelity assessment is proposed, which offers an overarching design for the ensuing experiment and research.

Chapter 4 introduces explicitly the experiment design, execution and rating process. Besides, the PA-based criterion for the assessment of information fidelity and categories of propositional correspondence are presented and justified for their application in dicussions of propostional correspondence distributions.

Chapter 5 is dedicated to the validation procedure of the PA-based criterion, against a conventional criterion for the assessment of information fidelity. Validation investigation is carried out on three dimensions: construct validity, criterion validity and rater reliability. To do so, statistical instruments such as SPSS and FACETS are employed for data analysis. Then, merits and demerits of the PA-based criterion will be discussed based on data analysis.

Chapter 6 starts with an exploratory attempt of discovering propositional correspondence pattern distributions to investigate examinees' performance in the message transfer, based on correspondence distribution data extracted from the PA-based information fidelity assessment. Some correspondence types are then put in SPSS with fidelity scores for correlation analysis. Later on, pedagogical implications of the investigation, such as incorporating PA into instructing information processing and peer review, are proposed.

Chapter 7 winds up the book by summing up major findings of the investigation, contributions to the related fields and limitations of the study in hope of offering some markers for future endeavors on this issue.

Chapter 2

A Review of Research on Interpreting Quality Assessment

Interpreting quality assessment has been in the play since the origin of interpreting. However, it did not thrive until after the World War Ⅱ, when the profession of interpretation started to gather attention. The profession needs codes of conducts and quality assurance to define qualifications for interpreters and their services. Furthermore, development of the profession requires a system of effective and plausible assessment instruments for interpreter training programs. In a globalized era, the ever-increasing personnel exchange in the world demands high quality standards for various interpreting service, namely "quality across the board" (Pöchhacker, 2016). Studies in these aspects typically fall into three categories: evaluation for professionals, assessment for interpreter trainees and measurement for interpreting researchers. The present study focuses on the study of trainees' performance evaluation, which concerns theoretical and empirical considerations in this aspect. In this chapter, different types of quality assessment in TIS are introduced, and then it moves on to a comprehensive review of major developments of types of quality assessment in TIS, followed by discussion on some key issues such as qualitative and quantitative methodologies, criteria and parameters. Finally, some major interpreter certification tests and their assessment criteria are presented.

2.1 Defining Quality in Interpreting

2.1.1 Quality in Interpreting

Quality has been a permanent concern across the fields of interpreting studies, but we do not have a universal or commonly agreed definition as to what quality in interpreting (QI) is exact, as it involves conceptual and dimensional complexity. Before the discussion of quality assessment/evaluation, we need to clarify qualifications of interpreters and the nature of QI, which could be traced some literature.

AIIC's manual defines a conference interpreter as follows:

A qualified specialist in bilingual or multilingual communication. He/She makes this communication possible between delegates of different linguistic communities at conferences, meetings, negotiations or visits, where more than one working language is used, by comprehending the concepts of the speaker's message and conveying them orally in another language, either in consecutive, simultaneous or whispering.

Besides carrying out a thorough preparation of the subject and terminology, a conference interpreter must possess a wide general knowledge in order to deal with all matters under discussion.

Conference interpreters are, moreover, bound to respect the code of professional ethics, including the strictest professional secrecy. (AIIC website: http://aiic.org/site/world/conference)

These paragraphs depict some major responsibilities that a conference interpreter undertakes: facilitation of communication, oral rendition of message, thorough preparation, possession of extensive knowledge and abiding to moral ethics. Although this is a definition to a conference interpreter, we can assume that qualifications also apply to interpreters in different settings.

Moser-Mercer, on the basis of AIIC's description, gives a definition to the concept of optimum quality:

> Optimum quality in professional interpreting implies that an interpreter provides a complete and accurate rendition of the original that does not distort the original message and tries to capture any and all extralinguistic information that the speaker might have provided subject to the constraints imposed by certain external conditions. (1996: 44)

AIIC and Moser-Mercer see quality from an idealistic perspective, which commonly defines ultimate performance expected of interpreting:

① accurate rendition of the original message;

② inclusion of all linguistic and extra-linguistic information;

③ natural performance against environmental constraints.

Different from Moser-Mercer, Grbić (2008) views interpreting service as a product in market. Rather than viewing quality as ideal or perfect performance, Grbić, following ISO definition, considers quality as "a common feature of the product that can (and must) be measured" (Pöchhacker, 2015:334), which varies with specific demands of customers.

In a third view, quality is represented by the excellence of performance extracting detected errors and mistakes in interpreting service. The extent of excellence is reflected by the number and types of errors detected, with an inverse proportion—the more errors found, the worse the QI is; the fewer errors found, the better the QI is. Scholars on error analysis choose their lenses from linguistic, paralinguistic and pragmatic perspectives. While there is optimal quality, an implication of perfect performance, we can depict the lowest level of quality "pessimal quality" on the basis of error analysis, representing that an interpreter fails to convey the linguistic and extra-linguistic message, where we could find the most typical and numerical errors to such an extent that the service is completely rendered unacceptable.

Both optimal quality and pessimal quality are extremes in the interpreting service, but they set up a space in between where QI could move around, as quality is not a fixed value in interpreting. It is a result of various variables in effect, and even a slight change of a factor could move quality to the other direction. Here is a model of continuum of QI (see Figure 2.1):

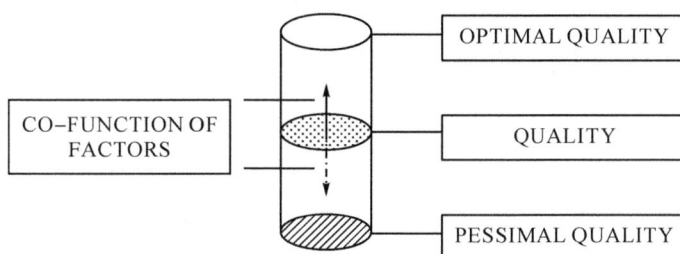

Figure 2.1 QI as a Continuum

But what are the factors that function in QI? What makes QI so complex? Routledge Encyclopedia of Interpreting Studies describes QI in this way:

> ... (quality) could be applied to all interpreting events across historical, cultural and social contexts. Multiple, and sometimes even contradictory, definitions highlight different aspects of quality, depending on the object of study (i.e interpreting in different settings or modes) as well as on the aims of a given study, its underlying epistemology and its theoretical approach. (Pöchhacker & Grbić, 2015: 334)

To better understand the conceptual complexity of QI, we need to explore its epistemological origin—conceptual complexity of interpreting, and its theoretical approach.

2.1.2 Interpreting as a Multi-Dimensional Service

Interpreting service is complex in nature, which involves various variables. A change of a certain variable will lead to a shift of interpreting mode and type. This multi-dimensional nature of interpreting is likely to result in various perceptions of interpreting quality among users and interpreters themselves. In other words, complexity of interpreting quality, to a large extent, derives from the multi-variable nature of interpreting service.

Kopczyński (1994) states that the key variables affecting interpreting include:

① setting;

② form;

③ content of message;

④ norms of interaction and interpretation;

⑤ participants.

He claims that interpreting is contextually determined. It complicates interpreting in that each variable will be weighed differently in different settings, when it comes to quality evaluation.

Pöchhacker (2015) further explores these variables and depicts a multi-faceted map in defining interpreting. The major typological parameters include:

(1) Setting

One of the earliest settings that would need interpreters is trading and business transactions, which is now business interpreting. Later on, interpreting performance developed to different spheres of social interaction. There arise diplomatic interpreting, military interpreting, court interpreting, educational interpreting and community interpreting (public service interpreting) (see Figure 2.2).

isclated contact   *institutionalized contacts*

EXPEDITION
          TRANSACTION
                              ADMINISTRATION

Exploration   Trade/Business
Warfare   Military
                         Diplomacy
Conquest
                                   (Colonial) Administration
                                       Law & Justice
          Missionary Work   Religous Services
              Scientific/Technical Cooperation
                                       Public Services
                         Media

INTER --------------------------------------- INTRA

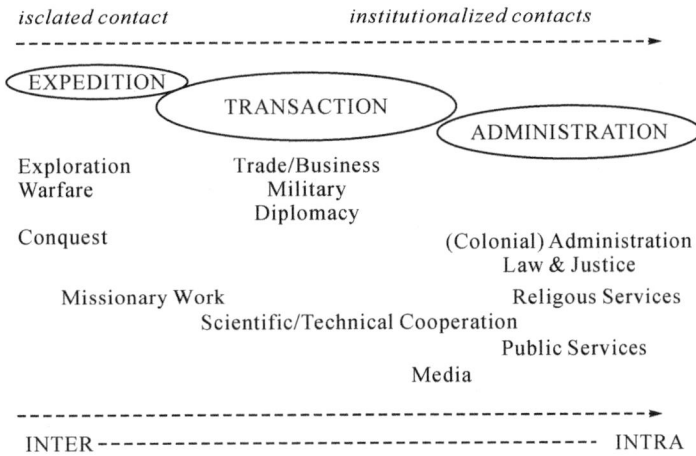

Figure 2.2 Interpreting in Different Social Context (After Pöchhacker & Grbić, 2015: 26)

Interpreting also varies according to the forms and formality of social interaction. There is dialogue/liaison interpreting for face-to-face/bilateral communication, conference interpreting for multilateral communication, as well as signed language interpreting for communication with disabled people (see Figure 2.3).

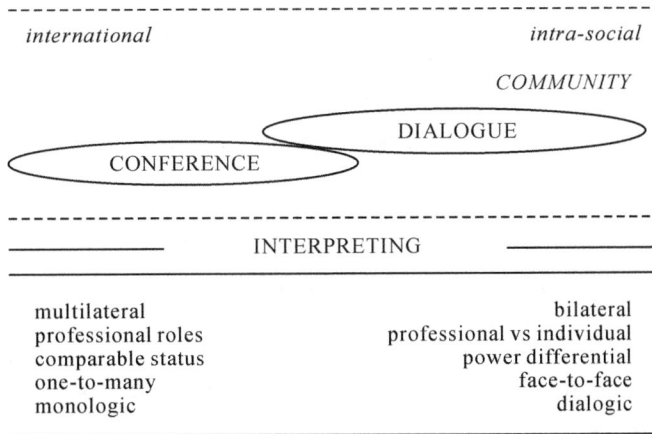

international   *intra-social*

                                   COMMUNITY

                          DIALOGUE
          CONFERENCE

                   INTERPRETING

multilateral   bilateral
professional roles   professional vs individual
comparable status   power differential
one-to-many   face-to-face
monologic   dialogic

Figure 2.3 Types of Interpreting (After Pöchhacker & Grbić, 2015: 27)

(2) Mode

With respect to the working mode, interpreting performance can be conducted with consecutive interpreting and simultaneous interpreting (SI), which could be further divided into sub-categories, as shown in Figure 2.4.

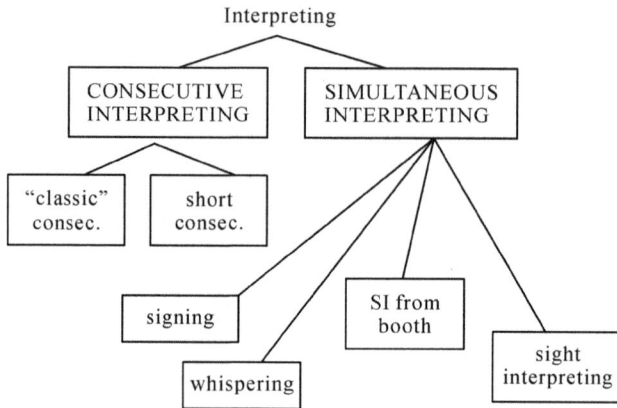

Figure 2.4 Modes of Interpreting (After Pöchhacker & Grbić, 2015: 29-30)

(3) Participants

Studies have revealed that quality viewed by the listeners is distinct from that by the interpreters themselves. The model of Communication Configuration (Gile, 1991) shows that participants consist of not only the interpreter and the users, but also the client or the manager who hires the interpreter. Besides, there are "bystanders" who are also interested in the interpreting service for analytical or educational purposes, such as interpreter trainees, teachers, colleagues or researchers. The relationships between the participants and perspectives are shown in Figure 2.5.

In addition to these factors, there are some others that deserve our attention, like directionality, discourse, use of technology, medium. They all are on the list of interpreting variables.

The conceptual complexity of interpreting leads to the conceptual complexity of quality in interpreting. Normally, quality in business interpreting is not viewed in the same way as quality in diplomatic interpreting, where formality and publicity issues would result in different expectations and evaluation criteria. Quality in consecutive interpreting is also seen differently from simultaneous interpreting, because messages are transmitted in different ways, and the appearance of interpreters is another issue for consideration. Lastly, perception discrepancies exist between users and clients, and even interpreters themselves hold different views.

Perspectives on Quality in Interpreting

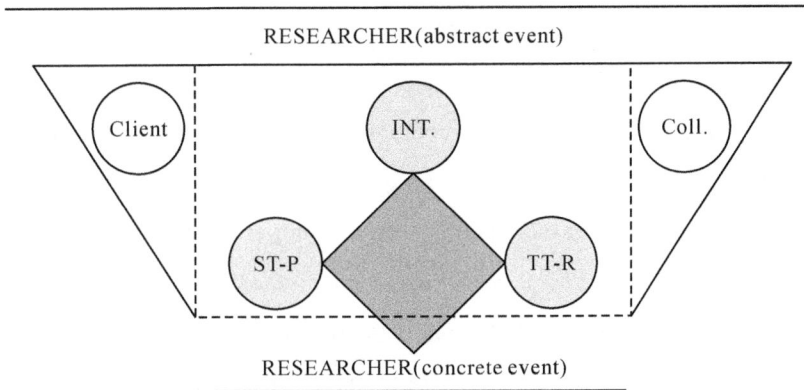

RESEARCHER(abstract event)

Client   INT.   Coll.

ST-P   TT-R

RESEARCHER(concrete event)

Figure 2.5 Participants on Quality in Interpreting (After Pöchhacker & Grbić, 2001: 412)

Note: ◆: communicative event; ST-P: source-text producer; TT-R: target-text receiver

2.1.3 Conceptual Complexity of QI

Conceptual complexity of QI derives from complexity of interpreting, which can be viewed from its research methods, perspectives and purposes.

First, interpreting quality could be seen in perspective, which requires different research methods for data elicitation and extraction. Researchers laying eyes on interpreting products would focus on audio-visual and textual analysis of recordings. Researchers from the perspective of translation process research (TPR) would explore mental and cognitive aspects of interpreters at work. Researchers from sociological perspective would be keen on interpreter-mediated interactions on the basis of ethnographical methods.

Second, the above-mentioned perspectives of interpreting quality studies serve different purposes. A product-oriented perspective means that researchers are keen on textual and linguistic features of interpreting performance. A process-oriented perspective means that researchers are eager to know what happens in the black box. A sociological perspective refers to the fact that researchers want to discover the communication effects and interpersonal relations.

These studies, examining interpreting quality from various perspectives with different research methods and purposes, would reveal certain aspects of multi-faceted interpreting quality to us. This result leads to some consequences. First, researchers from different perspectives would hold different notions of interpreting quality. Second, researchers with different research methods would have different outcomes when analyzing quality-related data, which would hold different standards to measure quality. Interpreting is a combination of cognitive, linguistic, cultural and social activities. Thus, focusing on any one or various aspects of these factors would lead to different assessment criteria. From different perspectives, researchers would need different research methods. For instance, TAP, retrospective protocols, interpreting diary would reveal decision-making process; for linguistic research, corpus and text-analysis methods like error analysis and propositional analysis are useful; for cultural and sociological research, questionnaire and survey are used frequently. With different perspectives of quality in mind, we will value quality with different criteria.

QI is also contextually and pragmatically bound. Situational variables might call for priorities in context. Kopczyński (1994) states that when defining QI, the following factors need to be taken into consideration:

① the speaker, his status and the status of his receptors;

② the speaker's intention in issuing the message;

③ the speaker's attitude toward the message and the receptors;

④ the receptor's attitude toward the message and the speaker;

⑤ the interpreter, his/her competence, judgments, attitudes and strategies, the form of the message;

⑥ the illocutionary force of the message;

⑦ the existing norms of interaction and interpretation of a speech community, the setting.

After analyzing the features and complexity of QI, it comes to sense that quality of interpreting performance, basically, is a continuum moving between optimal quality and pessimal quality, which easily lends itself to variables in effect. These variables should be taken into account to evaluate QI, especially when we evaluate QI for different purposes in different settings. With that in mind, let's now proceed to the next section of this chapter, which focuses on QI in different settings.

2.2 Review of Quality Assessment[①]

In this section, a brief review of research on QI will be presented on the basis of QI settings, namely QI assessment in professional and educational contexts. Professional interpreting includes conference interpreting and community interpreting, and assessment in educational contexts refers to assessing interpreter trainees' performance. (Pöchhacker, 2001; Bartłomiejczyk, 2007) The classification of professional and educational QI assessment is mainly because studies on these two aspects focus on various research topics and methodologies. Both QI assessments in professional and educational contexts will be analyzed from the perspective of conceptual issues and methodological issues.

2.2.1 Quality Assessment in Professional Contexts

QI assessment in professional contexts includes QI assessment of conference

---

① In interpreting studies, the terms "measurement, evaluation, assessment" are controversial and rarely defined, which are subject to personal perceptions. Moser-Mercer (1996) clarifies evaluation, assessment and measurement, based on the interpreting settings. With the classification, we evaluate professional interpreters' performance, measure interpreting performance for research purposes and assess interpreting performance for pedagogical reasons. The present study focuses on the trainees' performance. Assessment is used as a term for investigating quality hereinafter.

interpreting and community interpreting. Literature in this field centers around two significant themes—conceptual issues and empirical research, which are to be unfolded in this part of the section.

2.2.1.1 Conceptual Issues

When it comes to quality assessment, it is desirable to know how to quantify it. Carroll, in a study that sparkles the flame of systemic study of QI, raises several questions concerning quality assessment in translation and interpreting, of which answers have been sought after ever since:

> What is the criterion of success, that is, how can success in translation and interpretation be measured? In the case of translation, what kinds of measures of accuracy and effectiveness could be obtained? In the case of conference interpretation, could conference participants (not being able to understand the language from which the interpretation is made) provide any reliable and valid judgments of the success of the performance? Or could success be measured only by a detailed comparative analysis of the input and output messages? (1978:122)

What Carroll actually wants to know about comes down to three questions: What to assess with? Who are to assess? How to assess QI? Despite the holistic criteria provided by AIIC and Moser-Mercer, scholars are keen to assess QI with more specific standards and criteria. And these have been questions that numerous scholars are trying to provide answers to. Carroll's first two questions deal with conceptual issues of QI assessment, namely, assessment criteria and assessors.

Carroll's first question deals with contents of QI assessment. To conduct QI assessment, a priority is to get to know what to assess with. Research of this kind starts with discussion of assessment standards and criteria.

Inspired by an entrance examination for a translation and interpretation program, Carroll (1978) discusses translator and interpreter qualifications and methods for aptitude tests. He classifies T&I performance into four types: careful written translation, quick informal written translation, consecutive conference interpretation and simultaneous conference interpretation. He suggests that an aptitude test should take into account such as verbal intelligence, bilingual knowledge and cultural knowledge. Carroll stresses verbal intelligence in the study, including reading comprehension, vocabulary, general culture and education, fluency.

Carroll's study is the first of its kind in proposing qualifications for conference interpreting, which mainly concern the linguistic abilities of translators and interpreters. This qualitative study initiates systemic theoretical and empirical considerations on the issue of T&I quality.

Hearn, Chesher and Holmes (cited from Pöchhacker, 2001:414) are among the first to respond to Carroll's questions in practice. They ask 60 interpreters to evaluate two interpreter-mediated events, who consider bilingual knowledge, neutrality, socio-communication skills, responsibility, honesty, politeness and humility as important qualities of good interpreters.

Bühler (1986) proposes that criteria for the evaluation of interpreting service consist of two parts: linguistic (semantic) and extra-linguistic (pragmatic) criteria, on which basis a two-part questionnaire is designed for professionals' perception of QI. This study marks the beginning of evaluation from linguistic and extra-linguistic aspects in interpreting studies.

As for Bühler's followers, their work is to try to answer some basic questions raised by Moser:

—What constitutes good interpretation from the (professionals' or) users' point of view? Can an ideal interpreter be inferred from their replies?

—How do (interpreters or) users rank the importance of various quality criteria in interpretation? If ranked, are the rankings reliable and consistent?

—Do users' expectations vary markedly from one set of circumstances to another (different conference types) or do users have a basic set of expectations which prevail whatever the conference type? (1996: 146)

Altman (1990) conducts a study on factors that affect the quality of conference interpreting over two groups of professionals. Although the two groups disagree over the weight of some factors such as speed of delivery and accent, they reach the agreement that subject matter, quality of sound transmission are the two most important factors for interpreting performance. For professionals, specialized knowledge, language competence and cross-cultural awareness are the most needed in translation and interpreting schools.

Chiaro & Nocella (2004) conduct a research on a similar issue on over 200 interpreters across several continents, which is based on a two-part questionnaire similar to Bühler's. The ranking of criteria is similar to that of Bühler's, with consistency with original message, completeness of information and logical cohesion being the top three criteria. In terms of extra-linguistic criteria, concentration, preparation and teamwork ability are the top three.

Zhang (2011) surveys a total number of 24 interpreters serving in over 18 international conferences in China. He figures out that whatever the themes of the conferences, interpreters' expectations of service quality remain stable. However, importance attached to linguistic criteria (completeness of message, logical cohesion and terminology) varies with the change of themes. Professionals pay more attention to terminology and grammatical correctness in SI than in consecutive interpreting, and they care more about completeness of message, logical cohesion and terminology in consecutive interpreting than in SI. Finally, Zhang calls for a fine-grained design to evaluate QI with a multi-dimensional approach, taking all participants into consideration, so as to reach to a rational judgment.

In community interpreting, standards and criteria of QI assessment is formally stipulated in codes of ethics. Code of ethics defines the entry level, responsibilities and roles of interpreters. It regulates interpreting performance and offers standards for evaluating interpreting performance. By analyzing 16 codes of ethics across the world, Hale (2007) categorizes 3 broad areas that the Codes cover:

① interpreter's responsibility to the message, including accuracy, impartiality and confidentiality;

② interpreter's responsibility to the profession, including dress, punctuality and solidarity;

③ interpreter's responsibility to self as a professional, including professional development, role consideration, working conditions and remuneration.

Two criteria in the first area directly concern quality assessment, namely, accuracy and impartiality. Confidentiality concerns moral the standard of interpreter, rather than the quality of performance. In most of the Codes, accuracy means being faithful to the original utterance, but not a literal or verbatim rendition of the source utterance. Some distinguish faithful interpreting from literal interpreting, explicitly claiming that the deeper meaning of utterance be rendered.

Impartiality refers to a strict objectivity in interpreter's work, regardless of personal feelings, beliefs or interests. 11 of the 16 Codes clearly defines impartiality as: "interpreters shall not voice an opinion, solicited or unsolicited", "members shall not ... perform functions ... such as advocacy, counseling or improper disclosure of information", "members shall remain neutral, impartial and objective ... refrain from altering a message for political, religious, moral or philosophical reasons". These Codes regulate dos and don'ts to community interpreters, which serve as guidelines for interpreters at work, although in a vague and elusive way.

Scholars have called forth advancing recognition and awareness of the code of ethics in community interpreting (Berk-Seligson, 1990; Cambridge, 2000; Wallmach, 2002; Ibrahim, 2004; Shouten, 2012; Hlavac, 2017). There have been efforts in this aspect (Angelelli, 2004; Idh, 2004; Corsellis, et al., 2004; Hertog, et al., 2004), talking about the constructs and rationale of the Codes. However, these guidelines for interpreters cannot solve all the tricky situations that professionals encounter at work. Opinions are voiced out to study empirical application of the Codes, because it is equally important to get sufficient knowledge of how Codes apply to actual interactions. Only when theoretical and empirical considerations of the Codes are conducted can we have a thorough understanding of it. Furthermore, academic debates should be accompanied with practical training so as to ensure the quality of interpreting services. (Hale, 2007)

When taken into empirical consideration, Codes have taken its toll, due to vague and rough descriptors. There have been suspicions about validity and applicability of Codes to interpreter-mediated situations. Different perceptions of accuracy in community interpreting result in various expectations and assessing standards. In an interview with medical practitioners, Resera, Tribe & Lane (2015) find that practitioners prefer interpreters to process information rather than parrot, eliminating some unnecessary repetitions and unrelated babblings, possibly because of time constraints. On the contrary, studies through interviews show that legal participants (police officers, judges, lawyers) expect verbatim translation from interpreter. (Berk-Seligson, 1990; Mikkelson, 1998; Hale, 2004) Such expectations, as it is argued, are because that questioning in legal situations is conducted purposefully and tactically, and legal practitioners could evaluate the situations by observing and hearing the responses and answers, linguistically and para-linguistically. Rigney (1999) studies questioning in interpreted testimony through textual analysis. He points out that the linguistic manipulation of questions is a strategic tool of domination for practitioners, with interrogation performing different pragmatic functions. Interpreters who fail to realize this will alter the basic function of questions used for manipulation. With this failure, attorneys will lose control over the process. Clifford (2015) analyzes the dynamic values in medical interpreting, claiming that strictly following practitioner's and patient's utterance would face the risk of communication collapse, largely due to cultural-specific disparities. Codes of ethics require interpreter to be accurate in rendition. But when it comes to actual interactions, interpreters find that users have different expectations on different occasions, about which they could not find appropriate guidance from the Codes.

In sum, for QI assessment in professional contexts, numerous studies have offered insights for QI assessment criteria. Despite minor discrepancies, there seems to be a consensus that major assessment components include linguistic and extra-linguistic issues, among which accuracy, delivery and fluency are the top three components. These findings help establish the main constructs of assessment criteria in practice. Despite the achievements and progress, discussions in this aspect, even the existing codes of ethics, fail to clearly define accuracy, which is a determinant factor of assessing information fidelity.

Carroll's second question concerns assessors. It has been discussed in the previous section that participant is a variable in QI assessment that deserves special attention. Studies have shown that users and interpreters demonstrate various perceptions in QI assessment.

Some studies adopt Bühler's design to investigate users' criteria on interpreting quality, and some compare the criterion discrepancies between user group and interpreter group, offering insights of inter-group or intra-group variability. Kurz (1988) takes Bühler's criteria as reference to survey delegates to a medical conference in an attempt to test whether Bühler's assumption that critical quality indicators among interpreters is in line with those of users. It is found that some important criteria in professionals' group, such as accent, pleasant voice and grammar, are considered less important by the delegates, which confirms that user's perception of interpreting quality is different from professionals'.

Gile (1990) carries out a similar study on a medical conference, focusing on six elements of quality: general quality, linguistic quality, terminology, information fidelity, voice and delivery, and major problems. Gile, too, notices the inter-group difference in weights of voice in quality assessment, which is less significant among the user group.

Inter-group differences in evaluation criteria have aroused researchers' interest. The aforementioned studies help form an assumption that different groups of participants in different settings, with different scales of assessment, would view interpreting performance differently. To confirm that assumption, Kurz (1993) hypothesizes that different groups of end users have different expectations and needs. In this regard, a comparative study of three user groups is carried out. Also on the basis of Bühler's questionnaire, Kurz discovers that these three user groups reach consensus on top criteria, such as consistency with original message, logical cohesion, terminology and completeness. Still, three different user groups yield three different evaluation profiles. This study confirms that interpreting is characterized with "situationality and communicative context" (Kurz, 1993: 20), in which user group is an essential factor to be considered.

In China, Zhang (2011) carries out a relevant study intended to investigate the intra- and inter-group differences between interpreters and users. In the intra-group perspective, he realizes that interpreters are unexpectedly unanimous in service expectations, while user expectations vary with the subject matter, levels and modes of interpreting. From the inter-group perspective, Zhang concludes that interpreters possess higher standards than users, both in linguistic and extra-linguistic aspects.

While theoretical constructs of QI assessment for professionals are mainly established, most studies are still uni-dimensional; that is, studies are only focusing on prescriptive and subjective assessments of interpreting performance based on perception and survey. A serious challenge is to validate these theoretical constructs. In response, Pöchhacker (1994) proposes to conduct product-oriented research to build a multi-parameter model for descriptive analysis, counterpart to the prescriptive and subjective quality assessment of the service. He stresses that direct response from delegates and textual analysis of interpreting performance are complementing each other, when the quantity of quality-related features in text analytical approach reaches to a massive point.

2.2.1.2 Empirical Research

In addition to the conceptual discussions with QI assessment that are centering around theoretical constructs, there are product-oriented investigations based on empirical approach, focusing on specific elements of QI assessment.

Researchers use variable-based methods to study interpreting product, that is, to evaluate the product by quantifying data of some variables, in an objective way.

Error analysis (EA) has long been used in product analysis. Barik (1971) is a pioneer in applying error analysis to conference interpreting. He designs a coding scheme of meaning departures in SI from the perspectives of omission, addition and error. Each type of the scheme is divided into several parts according to the location of departures in the sentence. By analyzing instances of departures, he further classifies them into mild and serious ones, according to the degree of deviances from the original sentence. Barik handles the texts mainly on the lexical and phrasal levels, mainly literally, which has been questioned in that the linguistic and structural differences between the source text and the target text are neglected. Nevertheless, he paves the road for EA's application in textual and analytical studies of interpreting performance.

With references from cognitive and psychological linguistics, scholars realize that parameters like omissions and deletions are not crucial factors that affect QI. Instead, they are considered as outcomes of strategy use to cope with difficult situations when interpreters' cognition is fully loaded. The Effort Model and tightrope hypothesis offer the theoretical mechanism.

Napier (2004) considers the factors that lead to interpreters' omissions. Rather than classifying errors into deviants, Napier finds out that interpreters use omission in a strategic way, intentionally or unintentionally, dependent on their familiarity with the subject matter and the situation. The study confirms that omission should not be simply considered as interpreting fault or error, and it could be conscious strategic use to carry on the interpreting task smoothly. The findings shed light on a new perspective of discourse analysis beyond linguistic considerations.

Gile (2011) analyzes the SI product of President Obama's inaugural speech on TV. He detects three kinds of deviants of the SI products: errors, omissions and infelicities (EOIs). Gile finds that the large number of EOIs detected in the products is more of a cognition-saturated issue than a linguistic or extra-linguistic one, which he explains with SI tightrope hypothesis. Another finding is that there are more EOIs in English-Japanese SI than those in English-French and English-German SI shows that under high cognitive pressure, linguistic and language-pair specific idiosyncrasies do affect the quality in SI. Gile also believes that a naturalistic method of product analysis, which is also replicable, can be powerful in answering questions that are extremely difficult for experiments.

Wang & Gu (2014) follow Gile's trail in adopting EOIs to explore the factors behind interpreting problems. Factor analysis of the data shows that EOIs are mainly because of overloaded cognitive capacity, which is similar to that of Gile's study. It is suggested that in evaluating SI performance, variables such as interpreting competence, cognitive capability, norms of interpreting, and language specificity should be taken into consideration.

Zhang (2006) also links omissions in SI with the Effort Model, demonstrating that omissions in SI are interpreters' strategy in dealing with the source message, rather than errors. She analyzes the reasons for omissions in SI, explaining that minor omissions do not affect the quality.

Syntactic differences are another variable that is likely to exert influence upon QI. Wilss (1978) discusses the types of syntactic anticipations in SI under the co-effects of syntactic structures and context. Uchiyama (1991, 1992) explores the effects of word order and syntactic differences on English-Japanese interpreting. He analyzes the problems arising from the linguistic structures in terms of inanimate subjects and pre-modifying adjectives, with coping strategies given at the end. Wilss and Uchiyama focus on the potential problems caused by language-pair specificities, but they do not apply them in evaluation.

The above-mentioned studies concern the individual variables of interpreting products, conducting research in a naturalistic method, eliminating the limitations of experimentation. These studies also enhance our understanding of quality in conference interpreting with detailed analysis of "real" products, always in a seemingly objective and quantified way. However, it is noted that these studies focus on one aspect of interpreting product are isolated and unlikely to integrate into the undertaking of overall quality evaluation. Even though errors and omissions are detected, the classification seems to be subjective in a way, making the method less duplicable or applicable. And most of the studies focus on the lexical and syntactic equivalence of the product, ignoring semantic analysis, among other things.

To sum up, since the late 1970s, QI assessment in professional contexts has been gaining momentum, which center, around three major areas. The first area pertains to investigating the interpreters' perception of being an interpreter and good interpreting performance, always taking a holistic approach towards evaluation. Studies in this aspect start to establish a theoretical and analytical framework for future studies. The second area has to do with the investigation of users' perception of interpreting and quality criteria. The practices reveal some users' priorities in quality criteria different from interpreters', enriching our understanding of the multi-dimensional perception of quality evaluation. The third area marks product analysis, mostly with empirical studies. The practices mostly focus on one or more variables of fidelity or fluency of interpreting output, attempting to measure how these variables affect interpreting performance and evaluation, and a vast majority of them offer pedagogical implications. Taken together, these areas represent a developing awareness of the role that evaluation plays in interpreting research and training. As to China, it embarks on

QI research much later than the Western countries, but researches are mushrooming and contribute fresh and meaningful insights to the whole cause of QI.

Despite the achievements, there are still some issues awaiting concentrated attention. First, theoretical constructs of QI assessment have reached consensus, but these standards and criteria are controversial in practice. A majority of research findings point to a fact that accuracy (or information fidelity) is regarded as one of the most important criteria in QI assessment, but there is a lack of a clear definition and detecting method of information accuracy. The fuzzy concept of information accuracy could be partially blamed for the various, or even contradicting assessment outcomes among participants. Consequently, scholars call for a "standardized and feasible QI information assessment unit" (Cai, 2007:42), so as to avoid over-subjective assessment in this regard.

Another challenging task, among other things, concerns research methodology. QI-related studies are mostly isolated, lacking horizontal and vertical comparison and connection with other QI dimensions. While questionnaires and interviews are done with interpreters or users of CI, researchers fail to conduct product analysis to check whether the qualitative data could be triangulated with quantitative data. For researchers interested in product analysis, they ignore conducting questionnaires or interviews. The separation of qualitative and quantitative studies hampers the accomplishment of a standardized sheet of survey. The methodological considerations of quality evaluation are to be further discussed in Section 2.1.4.

2.2.2 Quality Assessment in Educational Contexts

Interpreting quality in educational contexts (e.g. interpreter training programs) is assessed differently from that in conference and community contexts in the sense that in the former case, quality is mostly measured through test-elicited assessment, while in the latter case, quality is measured and judged on the basis of field work. If we say that quality studies on professional performance are intended for norm construction, then studies on trainee performance mostly are meant for predictive and diagnostic purposes.

Assessment is an essential method to elicit data from testing. It is characterized with "a wide range of methods for evaluating pupil's performance and attainment including formal tests and examinations, practical and oral assessment, classroom-based assessment carried out by teachers and portfolios" (Gipps, 1994: vii). The portfolios mentioned in the definition include formative assessment, summative assessment and ipsative assessment according to the purposes. Formative assessment always lasts throughout the whole coursework and offers feedback from teachers or learners. Summative assessment, on the contrary, takes place at the end of the course and provides information of students' progress and course achievements. The last type, ipsative assessment, is committed by trainees' themselves, comparing their performance against previous ones. On the basis of Gipps' definition, Sawyer (2004) distinguishes the features of these three types of assessment in interpreting education (see Table 2.1):

Table 2.1 Formative, Summative and Ipsative Tests (After Sawyer, 2004: 107)

Formative	Time: during the course Assessor: instructor Results: grading/suggestions or feedbacks Purposes: feedback on coursework
Summative	Time: end of the course Assessor: instructor/judge Results: grading Purposes: students' progress, learning/teaching achievements
Ipsative	Time: during the course Assessor: peers/trainees themselves Results: feedback Purposes: self-evaluation, reflective learning

The three types of assessment are, most of the time, used in an integrated curriculum for different testing uses. (Arjona, 1984) In interpreter training programs, these tests are meant for different uses: When we need to admit students or place students in correspondence to their ability, we will have placement or aptitude tests; provided that we need to know about students' progress or provide feedback to their coursework, we will employ formative or diagnostic tests; when we want to know how students master the skills or the teaching effectiveness at the end of the course, we will have summative tests. These three types of tests correspond to the three levels of interpreting expertise and could serve as "developmental markers" for interpreter trainees.

From the point of instructors, assessment in educational context could be divided into two aspects: ① external assessment performed by instructor/researcher or peer assessment; ② self assessment by students themselves. These two distinct aspects are performed with different purposes: External assessment is to know about students' performance and expertise; self assessment is used as a training tool designed to enhance trainees' autonomy and learning strategies.

For both external assessment and self assessment, a central concern is a clear explication of assessment criteria, as it greatly ensures reliability of test results and exerts great influence on quality of trainees' performance. Therefore, some assessment sheets have been developed to analyze and grade trainees' performance (Schjoldager, 1996; Ackermann et al., 1997; Falbo, 1998; Kutz, 2005; Chen, 2003). We are to discuss some of the assessment sheets.

Schjoldager (1996) proposes four main criteria for interpreting assessment: comprehensibility and delivery, language, coherence and plausibility; loyalty. She further illustrates these four criteria with some specific questions. Comprehensibility mainly concerns information and cultural awareness, while delivery concerns gesture and articulation. Language is mainly related to grammatical mistakes and mispronunciations. What's more, she explains why each criterion is important and presents some typical errors as examples. Schjoldager's assessment sheet offers detailed explanation for practitioners to use. However, some criteria are overlapping and oversimplified, subject to confusion in practice. Criterion like loyalty is likely to cause controversy, as Schjoldager does not explicitly illustrate this point.

Chen (2003, 2004) offers a detailed assessment sheet for student interpreters on the basis of Bachman's Communicative Approach. In the sheet, criteria consist of three distinct parts: knowledge, skills and psychology. Knowledge includes entries such as pronunciation and vocabulary, textual and pragmatic competence. Skills include memory, public speaking and note-taking, etc. The sheet is inclusive as well as specific, which is more applicable in teaching practice and diagnostic tests rather than in summative tests, as skill part is more revealing and inspiring to instructors.

Many other scholars also design similar assessment sheets for interpreter training. Cai (2007), on the basis of previous assessment criteria, summarizes six basic elements: acceptability, conciseness, variety, promptness and technicality. She stresses that the weight of these criteria should vary with learning stages, which adapts to different needs and expertise development of interpreter trainees. Yang (2005) proposes a detailed assessment sheet, taking loyalty, delivery, language, and time control as four main criteria. Deng (2007) proposes a similar assessment sheet, which includes bilingual knowledge, encyclopedic knowledge, interpreting skills and psychological factors. Liu & Zhang (2009), based on the framework of communicative language ability and "test usefulness" principle, design an assessment sheet for final achievement test of interpreting. It contains key components such as information fidelity, delivery, language idiomaticity, interpreting skills, professional ethics and time control. Although these assessment sheets focus on various aspects of interpreting performance, there are several key elements that researchers agree upon: quality of language, information fidelity and professional ethics, with information fidelity being the most important criterion. These efforts contribute to interpreting assessment both theoretically and practically. However, it is argued that some criteria are vague enough to hamper the reliability of the test results. For instance, information fidelity is generally divided into loyalty, accuracy and completeness. But it is not clear to what extent interpreters' makeshift strategy could be viewed as being loyal to the original. Barik (1971) views deviation from original sense as interpreting errors, including omission, addition and deletion, but it is doubted whether assessing interpreting performance at lexical/phrasal level is plausible. Liu & Zhang (2007) defines loyalty as a correct expression of speakers' views and intentions, but they fail to describe exactly the way of telling speakers' information and intentions. When it comes to assessment, it's up to raters' preference and personal understanding to judge whether some deviations (addition, omission, deletion) are considered as being loyal to the original information. It falls into the trap of subjective judgment.

Interpreter tests, including performance tests, are also an important component of QI assessment in educational contexts, which inject theoretical constructs of assessment into practical use. Similar to QI assessment in professional contexts, criteria and scales of interpreting tests have been the foci of researchers and test designers.

Schojoldager (1996) proposes a four-criterion framework for instructors to offer feedback to trainees' performance, which includes comprehensibility and delivery, language, coherence and plausibility and loyalty. Riccardi (2002), on the basis of this framework, breaks down the four macro-criteria into 17 indicators of assessment, which include phonology, prosody, lexical and productive deviations, disfluency, eye contact and posture. Detailed as these indicators are, their practicality is much problematic. (Lee, 2008) These criteria are designed for formative tests; therefore, they do not have the rubrics to "translate interpreting performance into numerical scores" (Lee, 2008: 168).

Pöchhacker also recommends four criteria for interpreting assessment: accurate rendition, adequate target language expression, equivalent intended effect and successful communicative interaction. (2001: 413) This framework covers lexical and semantic equivalence and socio-pragmatic equivalence of interaction. However, it does not absolutely fit interpreter performance tests, as the framework focuses on "interpreting service quality, rather than product quality" (Lee, 2008:168).

To make up for the drawbacks of the above-mentioned criteria, Lee (2008) designs a rating scale for interpreting performance assessment, including accuracy, target language quality and delivery. Also, a band scheme, together with detailed descriptors, is proposed to assess examinees' interpreting performance.

Similarly, Lee (2015) proposes an analytical scheme for consecutive interpreting performance assessment, which includes content, form and delivery. Different from Lee (2008), who adopts a top-down research method, Lee (2015) adopts a bottom-up method. By combing through previous related criteria for interpreting performance assessment, he picks out 42 criteria. Then, by means of survey, 22 criteria are retained to construct a draft rating scale that is used for further validation. Furthermore, each criterion is given a weighted score on the basis of scoring results.

Han (2015) proposes a three-criterion framework, covering information completeness, fluency of delivery and target language quality. Further, he suggests that in addition to the scale design, interpreting performance assessment should also focus on some other major aspects: raters, rating procedure and reporting of assessment outcomes. And he stresses the necessity of validation of criteria for interpreting tests.

These discussions with interpreting performance test designs and criteria push forward theoretical development in this aspect, which is a great boost for practical interpreting tests.

To conclude, QI assessment in educational contexts centers on interpreter trainees. Whether in external evaluation or self-evaluation, an eternal topic has been the development of interpreter performance tests. Test criteria and scales have been the foci of studies in this area; it has been widely accepted that interpreting test should elicit performance with several key criteria: information fidelity, delivery and target language quality.

Despite the hard-won consensus, one thing is still noticeable: Scale-based assessment is still questioned in terms of its subjectivity and lack of standardized information assessment unit (Cai, 2007), especially in the assessment of information fidelity, a top priority of QI assessment. To minimize the effect of subjectivity and enhance the reliability of interpreting test, researchers turn to computational approaches to apply data-driven assessment. Mackintosh (1983) uses a semantic scoring scheme to measure trainees' performance, validated by means of inter-rater reliability. Scholars (Tommola & Lindhom, 1995; Lee, 1999; Tommola & Helevä, 1998) also suggest propositional analysis be used to evaluate the quality of interpreting performance, focusing on the semantic equivalence of information. They point out that propositional analysis offers a promising way for the analysis of the ideational and informational content.

2.2.3 Methodological Issues

For studies on quality in interpreting, researchers prefer to adopt various qualitative and quantitative methods for quality assessment studies in different interpreter-mediated interactions, depending on the purposes and settings of studies. In this section, a summary of methodological issues employed in interpreting studies of different settings will be presented.

2.2.3.1 Survey

Survey is mostly conducted with questionnaires or interviews, trying to figure out attitudes and views towards issues in question from one or more perspectives of the interaction (cf. Figure 1.3). The themes in this regard concern perception of participants, quality criteria, and qualifications of interpreters.

For conference and community interpreting, survey is considered to be one of the best ways to find out participants' satisfaction/perception with interpreting service. Bühler (1986), Kurz (1989), Kopczinski (1994), Hale (2007) and

Christensen (2011) conduct their research from the user perspective. They lay their eyes on the following variables: content accuracy, terminology, delivery, rhetorical skills, voice and pronunciation. Meanwhile, Ballantyne (2010), Vargas-Urpi (2015) and Hlavac (2017) turn to interpreters' perception of interpreting criteria and assessment. Zhang (2011) and Feinauer & Lesch (2011) compare user expectations with interpreter perceptions of interpreting quality, trying to find out the inter-group disparity. In educational contexts, questionnaire is conducted among the group of assessors (Ng, 2003) and the group of trainees.

Survey through questionnaire is a convenient and objective method of gathering data representative of a large group of target population. However, researchers need to be very careful with critical elements: sampling, instrument, procedure, and the response rate. (Liu, 2010) All these factors, if not dealt with care, will greatly undermine validity and reliability of the research.

Another issue that attracts attention of survey designers has been raised by Strong & Fritsch Rudser (1992)—subjective evaluation through surveys of perception provides useful insights for interpreting assessment, yet it should be accompanied with more objective measures of product analysis. It seems to suggest that "risk of systematic personal or contextual bias" (Pöchhacker, 2001) is a methodological limitation of survey research. This interactive observational research should be in joint work with non-reactive observational research, which mostly focuses on textual analysis of interpreting output. Textual analysis stresses variables like accuracy and adequacy, mostly applied in experimental studies. A mixture of textual analysis and survey method could make up for the drawbacks of these two methods when they are used alone.

2.2.3.2 Experimentation

Experimental research is a method of studying the effect of A on B. Normally, researchers manipulate one or more variables (A) to determine its/their effects on other variables (B). Different from the inductive characteristic of qualitative research, experimentation is deductive. A quantitative characteristic of experimental research is that variables can be measured or counted, that is, "by identifying, isolating and eliminating or introducing a range of variables, it is possible to ascertain the extent of impact on the 'thing' being investigated" (Hale & Napier, 2013:151).

Since the 1960s, experimental research on interpreting has focused on the impact of input parameters (speed, noise, accent, rhetoric) on interpreting performance. This method explores a new way for researchers to find out how interpreters perform under certain circumstances, offering fresh insights for quality assessment. This method also highlights a measurement of accuracy. Parameters of accuracy in interpreting have been many: error analysis (Barik, 1971; Bartłomiejczyk, 1999); informativeness and comprehensibility (Gerver, 1971); propositions and verbal accuracy (Mackintosh, 1983; Tommola and Lindholm, 1995; Tommola & Helevä, 1998; Yeh, 2015). In these experiments, researchers use counts or scores to define how well interpreters perform, although it is doubted that these parameters only cover one or two aspects of interpreting quality, if they cover any at all. (Pöchhacker, 2001) Barik (1971) and Mackintosh (1983) both admit that their scoring systems are by no means a comprehensive or gross way of quality assessment, since other factors such as delivery, intonation, pausing and idiomaticity are also critical. Nevertheless, these experiments, aiming at detecting and locating measurement indicators of performance, offer concrete and objective data that advance our understanding of quality criteria in interpreting.

2.2.3.3 Corpus-Based Studies

Corpus-based translation and interpreting studies have thrived since 1993, when Mona Baker published her pioneering work—*Corpus Linguistics and Translation Studies: Implications and Applications*. As a brand-new paradigm in TIS, corpus-based studies are based on authentic and objectively observed linguistic phenomena. The studies yield findings from quantitative research through analysis of the phenomena, processes and products of translation and interpreting.

In contrast to survey-based studies, work on corpus-based studies targeting interpreting quality is occasional. Cokely (1992) establishes a corpus of ten sign language interpretations in a conference to study interpreting errors. Pöchhacker (1994) uses corpus to examine quality-related features such as paralinguistic markers and coherence. Kalina (1998) establishes authentic and experimental corpora to research intonation, interference, errors and self-corrections.

As for the application of corpus in educational context, studies now are centering around theoretical discussions. Zhang (2009, 2011), Chen & Fu (2014), Wang & Li (2015) summarizes the development of corpus technology in interpreting studies, and explores the technicality and theoretical foundations of the establishment of corpus. Wen, Liang & Yan (2005) builds an interpreting corpus based on trainees' performance in TEM-8. Some Chinese researchers, such as Dai (2011), Li (2012, 2016) base their studies on this corpus to study para-language markers and prefabricated trunks of Chinese learners. It is generally acknowledged that corpus-based studies provide abundant, detailed and objective data for us, which, to a large extent, complements with earlier qualitative studies. However, researchers should be aware of its drawbacks, as "observational studies based on authentic textual corpora alone will be insufficient to the task of evaluating interpreting quality in concrete communicative interactions" (Pöchhacker, 2001: 419). It is suggested that a mixed qualitative and quantitative research method would greatly boost validity.

Admittedly, corpus-based interpreting studies have gained less momentum than corpus-based translation studies. A main reason lies in technical hurdles. Data processing in corpus-based interpreting studies involves collection, transcription, annotation and alignment, etc. Despite that, theoretical discussions and empirical efforts in this aspect have gained some progress and will play an increasingly important role in interpreting studies.

The choice of research methods depends on the research topic and intentions. Each method, when used alone, has its merits and demerits. But a combination of research methods could make full use of these methods and avoid potential drawbacks. A challenge that researchers in QI assessment encounter is that they always adopt one method and ignore others. For survey designers, if their research completely relies on survey results, they would find it hard to confirm their findings without conducting product analysis. For experimenters, if they devote themselves to empirical research without paying attention to surveys or interviews, they would miss an opportunity of triangulation that would validate their findings from a cognitive or psychological perspective. Furthermore, if subjects of experiment are of small size, reliability of findings would be severely undermined. Therefore, in research design, it is necessary to integrate research purposes with appropriate research methods or method portfolios, making a full play of the merits of each method, while eliminating possible drawbacks or shortcoming.

2.3 Information Fidelity

2.3.1 Defining Fidelity in Interpreting

Fidelity, referred to as "faithfulness, accuracy of a description, translation, etc." (Collins COBUILD), has been a key theme of translation and interpreting studies since the earliest stage and has always been regarded as a central instrument in assessing translation and interpreting quality. Fidelity, accuracy or faithfulness, according to Seleskovitch (1978), refers to the degree of achieved communicative effects through interpreting in comparison with the effects achieved among native listeners.

Information fidelity is considered to be multi-dimensional, which transcends linguistic equivalence to semantic and pragmatic equivalence. *Encyclopedia of Interpreting Studies* illustrates a connotative difference between faithfulness and fidelity. Contemporarily, faithfulness refers to accuracy and completeness of interpreting. Fidelity, on the other hand, involves the semantic elements and reliability of interpreting. Interpreting fidelity does include not only the content, but also the message pragmatically, which is "achieved through linguistic and paralinguistic choices made for their impact in a particular context and situation" (Pöchhacker, 2015:162). Setton & Dawrant (2016) proposes "basic fidelity", a bottom-line requirement for interpreter to convey basic communicative intent, without major mis-presentation or distortion. In this regard, the assessment of information fidelity should be more semantically and pragmatically than linguistically and para-linguistically involved. This multi-dimensional character of fidelity could also be seen in Canadian Code of Ethics of the Association of Visual Language Interpreters of Canada (AVLIC): "Fidelity of interpretation includes an adaptation to make the form, the tone, and the deeper meaning of the source text felt in the target language and culture." Hale claims that fidelity in interpreting is "a translation which takes into account the whole discourse and reproduces the intention and impact of the original"(2007: 116).

Thus, information fidelity refers to message or meaning equivalence in linguistic, semantic and pragmatic aspects between source utterance and interpreted utterance. Assessment of information fidelity, likewise, should consider linguistic, semantic and pragmatic effects of interpreted utterance.

Meanwhile, it is the multi-dimensionality of information fidelity that imposes great difficulty on the assessment of information fidelity. It is difficult to conduct analytical assessment on fidelity, for the reason that assessors, when conducting the assessment of information fidelity, are very unlikely to be free from the influences of other elements. (Gile, 2009) Despite the complexity, there are still efforts to assess fidelity in an analytical way, namely, assess the dimensions respectively, especially when it comes to interpreting tests and training.

2.3.2 Assessing Information Fidelity

Assessing information fidelity is much more difficult than defining it, as it involves feasibility and practicality of the criteria and scales.

Any attempt to circumscribe fidelity in a prescriptive sense must consider what criterion is possible or desirable—faithfulness to the letter or the spirit, to the speaker's words or to his or her (intended) meaning. The non-isomorphism of languages clearly makes surface linguistic equivalence incompatible with fidelity to ideas and sense. However, the need for ASSESSMENT naturally creates pressure for some consistent and verifiable yardsticks for correspondence between elements of source and target texts. (Pöchhacker, 2015: 162)

On the one hand, fidelity could not be assessed with linguistic equivalence alone. On the other hand, assessment needs clarified and measurable parameters and criteria to ensure reliability. The debate over whether information fidelity could be assessed independently or not results in two different ways of assessment: holistic method considering fidelity as a part of intrinsic whole quality; and analytical method considering information fidelity as an essential construct which could be assessed apart from other components.

2.3.2.1 Holistic Approach

Holistic assessment takes information fidelity as a part of whole quality. Convenient as it is, rater reliability is a constant concern. Studies that adopt the holistic assessment approach (Kurz, 1993, 2001; Gile, 1999) conclude with different outcomes. Gile (1999) states that there are perhaps two reasons for the outcome discrepancy. First, interpreting service users are not all bilinguals. They lack the expertise and linguistic competence required to assess interpreting performance, including information fidelity. Second, users of QI assessment, including some professionals, are prone to bias for or against a certain aspect of interpreting performance, for instance, voice or delivery. This "halo effect" would undermine the reliability of assessment outcomes. The discrepancy of assessment outcomes even exists among professionals or instructors, which derives from lacking precisely defined standards and instructions. (Gile, 1999; Pöchhacker, 2015)

Apart from QI assessment in professional contexts, holistic method could not fully serve the purpose of QI assessment in educational contexts. Assessing trainees' interpreting performance does not only serve the purpose of score rating, but also provide explicit information about trainees' competence trajectory and instruction feedback. It is desirable that QI assessment could elicit examinees' detailed information in various aspects, so as to offer insights for expertise development and detect prominent problems. Apparently, holistic assessment could not adequately fulfill such tasks.

2.3.2.2 Analytical Approach

As to analytical assessment of information fidelity, researchers center around measuring error analysis/deduction and criterion-referencing (using scales of descriptors to describe performance). (Turner, et al., 2010) Criterion-referencing is mainly used in diagnostic and formative tests. Error analysis (EA) and propositional analysis are two assessment tools employed in the assessment of information fidelity.

2.3.2.2.1 Error Analysis

Error analysis is firstly proposed in second language acquisition (SLA), which holds the notion that errors are "breaches of the code, signs of an imperfect knowledge of the code" (Corder, 1973: 295), "unsuccessful bits of language" (James, 2001:1), and "faulty use of a linguistic item in the eyes of a fluent or native speaker" (Richards & Platt, 2002:159). Error analysis intends to find out what errors are most likely to occur and the reasons behind these errors, and consequently shed light on language acquisition mechanism and suggest for prevention of such errors. Error analysis, according to Corder (1974), follows four steps: error identification, description, explanation and evaluation. Later on, EA goes beyond the realm of SLA and spreads to other linguistic branches, including translation and interpreting studies.

EA started to attract attention in interpreting studies in the late 1960s. Gerver (1969) classifies students' errors into omission, substitution and correction to study the effects of source language (SL) presentation rate on the performance of simultaneous interpreters. Instead of meaning equivalence, Gerver detects errors lexically. For instance, omissions are classified by words, phrases and word numbers, etc.

Barik (1971, 1975) is another pioneer in introducing EA into the assessment of information fidelity in interpreting studies. He examines information fidelity by means of a coding scheme of omissions, additions, substitutions and errors in simultaneous interpreting. Like Gerver, Barik detects these parameters mostly on the basis of lexical equivalence of the source and target texts. It is argued that lexical equivalence in his research could not fully reveal the picture of meaning.

Kopczyński (1983) moves a step further by considering errors as linguistic deviations from the target language and utterance deviations that hamper the communicative effects. Compared with Barik's definition of error, Kopczyński's definition considers pragmatic equivalence of interpreting. All the inaccuracies should be taken into account under a given set of circumstances.

Altman (1994) also employs a coding scheme of errors (omission, addition, inaccurate rendition of lexical items, and inaccurate rendition of longer phrases). Based on this scheme, Altman proposes a hierarchy of recurring errors from the least to the most, according to the degree of deviation. This hierarchy includes:

① excessive concentration on a preceding item due to processing problems, resulting in a lack of attention and hence omission;

② attempt to improve TL style, leading to a tendency to overstate the case or to embroider the text unnecessarily;

③ difficulty in finding the correct contextual equivalent for a given lexical item;

④ drawing erroneously upon one's store of background/general knowledge;

⑤ compression of two information items into one, thereby producing a third incorrect item;

⑥ shortcomings in mastery of the FL, leading to misunderstandings and therefore misinterpretations of the original speech. (1994: 34)

Gile (1999, 2011) uses errors, omissions and infelicities (EOI) to investigate "tightrope hypothesis" and cognitive saturation. Wang & Gu (2015) adopt Gile's method and study information fidelity of a live SI on TV with different language pairs. They firstly break the texts down into sense groups and compare errors, omissions and infelicities of the source text and the target text. They conclude that errors are largely due to language specificity. However, like Gile, they fail to explain explicitly the rationale behind their coding scheme, why and how they adopt these three criteria as EA parameters.

These studies make some first attempts to conduct EA in the assessment of information fidelity. Researchers propose and make use of their designed coding schemes mostly at lexical level. Even if they claim to stress semantic meaning, they base their studies on lexical equivalence, rather than laying eyes on semantic level. Secondly, these schemes largely depend on researchers' personal or subjective assessment, lacking an agreed definition of what it contains and how it is measured. This results in a heavy criticism towards its validity and reliability. In view of this, some scholars turn to linguistics for theoretical and practical references, with propositional analysis being one of them.

2.3.2.2.2 Propositional Analysis

Due to the fact that EA could not fully represent information fidelity in QI assessment, propositional analysis appears as an alternative. (Tommola and Lindholm, 1995) In addition to error counts, PA considers propositional accuracy as well.

PA develops a coding scheme of information equivalence, on the basis of propositional correspondence between the source text and the target text, whereby it quickly finds its use in analyzing interpreting performance. Mackintosh (1983) designs a complex semantic scoring scheme to study the quality of message transfer in relay interpretation. Although she does not mention propositional analysis, she clearly lays the foundation for future studies of fidelity in interpreting from the perspective of semantics.

Setton (2000) discusses PA as a methodological issue in interpreting studies. He points out that linguistics offers models of speech at various levels of meaning: morpho-phonological analysis, lexical-syntactic representation, logical-semantic representation and speech acts of discourse. Lexical-syntax represents meaning representation at the first level. This level of representation could not reflect the symbolic or logical notations of discourse, making it difficult for the listeners to get holistic meaning of the discourse. This is where logical-semantic representation comes in. He illustrates that PA, a tool for logical-semantic analysis, turns out to be analytic enough for a useful text-to-text comparison. This paper paves the way, in theory, for the applicability of PA in assessing information fidelity in interpreting performance.

Empirical studies are also carried out to apply PA into interpreting studies. Earlier experiments have indicated that PA is a relatively direct and reliable scoring instrument. (Tommola & Lindholm, 1995; Tommola & Helevä, 1998) Tommola and Helevä (1998) employ a PA coding scheme to investigate how information density and conceptual complexity of the source text could influence interpreting performance. They test the usability of propositional accuracy score in interpreting studies and conclude that PA seems to be suitable for analysis of source and target semantic contents.

These researchers employ PA as a tool to analyze information fidelity, with the assumption deep in mind that proposition is a reliable assessment unit. Yeh's research (2015) seems to be the first one to attempt to validate PA in the assessment of information fidelity. Combining Corder's error scheme (1974) with Kitntsch & van Dijk's proposition classification (1978), Yeh proposes a set of propositional errors for interpreting assessment, who investigates feasibility of PA in assessing information fidelity directly. By exploring inter-rater reliability of the PA-based assessment, he confirms the hypothesis that PA is feasible in assessing information fidelity.

In sum, scholars have mentionted that PA is feasible in QI assessment, both theoretically and empirically. (Tommola & Lindholm, 1995; Tommola & Helevä, 1998; Yeh, 2015) It offers not only a basic information assessment unit, but also a measurable and quantifiable way for the assessment of information fidelity, mitigating long-time-criticized subjectivity in QI assessment. In the meantime, the fact that PA focuses on logical and semantic meaning means that it can help avoid a lexical-equivalence assessment, which has been long awaited by interpreting researchers.

2.4 Summary

In this chapter, it depicts an outline of general situations of research on quality in interpreting, quality assessment and methodological application, theoretically and empirically. A more detailed review of QI assessment in professional and educational contexts is offered. Also, research on information fidelity, as a first descriptor of quality assessment, is briefly reviewed, stressing its assessment in educational context.

Interpreting quality is a multi-dimensional concept, which arises from the very multi-dimensional nature of interpreting itself. In addition to interpreter's output, assessment of interpreting quality should also take into account context, situation and user perspectives. The multi-perspective consideration of assessment makes it even more complex in practice. Typically, it lacks clear and clarified guidance and way of measurement.

Despite these drawbacks, researchers have committed great efforts into this undertaking. For QI assessment in professional contexts, it is often examined by users, interpreters themselves and participants. Early researchers pay attention to assessment constructs, paving the way for further study in this aspect. Later on, follow-up researchers lay their eyes on justifying these constructs and explore this field with sub-category criteria and measurable parameters. Some are not satisfied with a single-perspective evaluation that they compare user-and-interpreter perception of interpreting quality, in an effort to advance our understanding of quality assessment.

Quality assessment in educational context employs a portfolio of tools, dependent on the purposes and learning stages. It is required that quality assessment in this context be concrete, measurable and reliable. A typical example is the criteria and scale design of ATI (Assessment of Translation and Interpreting). Despite a growing number of studies on assessment criteria, currently, test measurement is still controversial, leading to unstable rater reliability. On the other hand, there is a gap between interpreting tests and interpreting training. Data elicited from tests are rarely noticed or studied by instructors, much less offer suggestions for adaptive or formative instructions.

When it comes to interpreting tests, it requires measurable and quantifiable criteria and parameters. Theoretical discussions in this aspect result in different proposals, because of various theoretical dimensions. However, of the several studies that discuss practical assessment criteria, researchers seem to reach consensus on some key criteria: information fidelity, language accuracy, fluency and communicative efficacy. Minor differences exist in the weighted scores assigned to these parameters. ATIs are the beneficiaries of these discussions, whose descriptors/assessment sheets are designed on the basis of these criteria. Still, a further scientific development of ATIs requires more specifically described and regulated descriptors/sub-criteria. Specifically, the assessment of information fidelity is still lacking a measurable way of assessment. This is likely to undermine inter- and intra- rater reliability of tests.

Methodologically, researchers have been tentative in their choice of research tools, adaptive to their research purpose. Frequently deployed research methods, such as surveys, interviews and experiments, while contributing to the epistemological establishment of quality assessment, also contain some demerits. It is pointed out that a research method alone could only solve a single problem or problems of one kind. But interpreting is complex in nature. We cannot expect a once-and-for-all research method to analyze all interpreting issues. All in all, the concept of quality cannot be pinned down to some linguistic substrates but must be viewed also at the level of its communicative effect and pragmatic meaning. These research methods have distinguishing merits and demerits. A possible way to eliminate their limitations is mixed methods, combing two or more approaches in one study. Researchers can work on mutually enriching exchange of methodological tools.

Traditionally, assessment in educational contexts is detached from interpreter training. Descriptors of information fidelity are vague. Research in this regard is also limited in number and size. Looking into the future, large-sized research attempts in objective assessment of information fidelity should render complements to the current methodological package of interpreting assessment and more significantly, linguistics-referenced theories. Analytical assessment approach is considered capable of analyzing data elicited from interpreting tests, which are inspirational to adaptive instructions. EA and PA are two instruments for fidelity analysis in this kind. While error analysis finds it hard to fully represent information fidelity of interpreting performance, PA offers an alternative. More importantly, PA has the potential to facilitate interpreting education, which is a much-wanted function by instructors and researchers. As a central issue of this investigation, propositional analysis, together with a brief review of its development, is introduced in the next chapter.

Chapter 3

Propositional Analysis and the Assessment of Information Fidelity

In the previous chapter, propositional analysis is considered to be a promising tool for textual analysis in interpreting studies. The concept of proposition first comes out as a psychological term to represent meaning in memory. Later linguists adopt it as a tool to analyze semantic meaning of texts. The nature of proposition as a representation of meaning[①], regardless of language formality, shares some common grounds with the ideas of deverbalization and information processing in interpreting. In this chapter, a review of propositional analysis in linguistic and T&I studies will be presented, in an attempt to explore, theoretically, the feasibility of PA in the assessment of information fidelity of interpreting. In the latter part of this chapter, a theoretical framework of PA for the assessment of information fidelity is to be proposed, laying a foundation for empirical work of the study.

---

① In a wide sense, Leech (1974) classifies meaning into seven types: conceptual meaning, connotative meaning, social meaning, affective meaning, reflected meaning, collocative meaning and thematic meaning. In a narrow sense, Fillmore (1971) defines meaning on the basis of semantic properties of speech acts (cf. Table 3.1), which represents relations of predicate and arguments. For assessment purpose, the study adopts Fillmore's definition of meaning, which focuses on logical and relational analysis of propositional information.

3.1 Proposition

3.1.1 Defining Proposition

During the 1960s and 1970s, psychologists developed some psychological processing theories to describe the use and acquisition of knowledge and the comprehension and memorization of semantics. The foremost of its kind is a propositional theory for the representation of meaning in knowledge and memory. In this sense, proposition deals with the psychological representation of meaning, or, the meaning of concepts with respect to certain semantic memory. (Kintsch, 1974)

The concepts that Kintsch refers to underlie a hierarchy of meaning representation. The hierarchical structure, from the bottom to the top, includes word concepts, propositions and text base (see Figure 3.1):

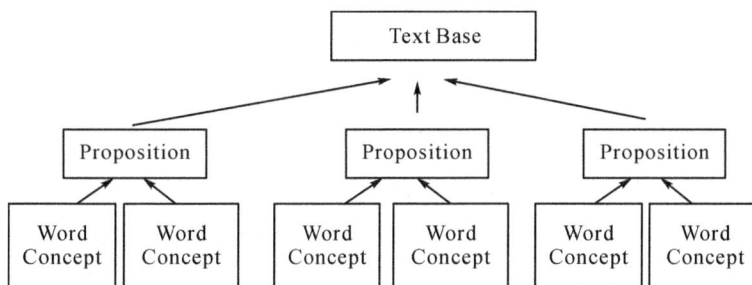

Figure 3.1 **Hierarchical Structure of Meaning Representation**
(**Based on Turner & Greene, 1977**)

Meaning representation is a lexical representation of what the author wants to deliver. An important subset of it is the lexicons, or the words used in texts. The entries of the lexicon are word concepts. Word concepts are abstract, expressed as words or phrases at the lexical-grammatical level. To distinguish word concepts and words, it is note-worthy that "(word concepts) have a completely different theoretical status. For each word concept there is a lexical description that specifies its meaning and use" (Kintsch, 1974:10). In addition, word concepts are abstract, represented by lexicons (words) in terms of linguistic information. Besides, word concept contains relationship of lexical items, defining reference to other words. Thus, word concept is not always reflected by a one-word lexicon. It may contain several words.

A proposition consists of at least two word concepts. One is "Predicate", and the other(s) "Argument(s)". Predicate defines a relation. The relation is a connection between a set of arguments forming a single idea. So, proposition is regarded as a basic unit of information in semantic memory. Examples are given in Table 3.1:

Table 3.1 Examples of Proposition

Sentence	Proposition	Predicate	Argument 1	Argument 2
John comes.	(COME, JOHN)	COME	JOHN	
The man is sick.	(SICK, MAN)	SICK	MAN	

Turner & Greene (1977) classify propositions into three groups, based on the types of relation they represent: predication, modification, and connection. Each group has distinguishing constraints to decide what arguments may be contained by the relation in forming a proposition.

Predicate proposition: ideas of actions or states. The relations are usually verbs. Predicate proposition also includes nominal proposition and references. Examples are given in Table 3.2:

Table 3.2 Examples of Predicate Proposition

Sentence	Proposition	Predicate	Argument 1	Argument 2
Smith eats an apple.	(EAT, SMITH, APPLE)	EAT	SMITH	APPLE
I am starving.	(STARVE, I)	STARVE	I	

Modifier proposition: restricting or limiting a concept with another concept. Negation is considered as a modifier proposition. Examples are given in Table 3.3.

Table 3.3 Examples of Modifier Proposition

Sentence	Proposition	Predicate	Argument 1	Argument 2
Mike dented the car's bumper.	1. (DENT, MIKE, P2)	DENT	MIKE	P2
	2. (POS., BUMPER, CAR)	POS.	BUMPER	CAR
Jay does not play the piano.	1. (PLAY, JAY, PIANO)	PLAY	JAY	PIANO
	2. (NEGATION, P1)	NEGATION	P1	

Note: P1 = Proposition 1; P2 = Proposition 2

Connective proposition links propositions or facts to each other. Sometimes, this proposition may be left unexpressed, but must be inferred in analysis. Propositions of this kind is of essence to make a text cohesive. Examples are given in Table 3.4.

Table 3.4 Examples of Connective Proposition

Sentence	Proposition	Predicate	Argument 1	Argument 2
Richard and Huan are skiing.	1. (AND, RICHARD, HUAN)	AND	RICHARD	HUAN
	2. (SKI, P1)	SKI	P1	
The water is cold. So is the air.	1. (COLD, WATER)	COLD	WATER	
	2. (COLD, AIR)	COLD	AIR	
	3. (SO, P1, P2)	SO	P1	P2

A proposition is often embedded as arguments in other propositions. In particular, the arguments of connective propositions tend to be other propositions.

Propositions do not work alone but are connected to form a cohesive text base. Proposition is considered as a single unit of semantic information, and a text base, the combination of propositions, represents the meaning of a whole text. It contains all the necessary information and elements to derive a complete natural discourse. The constructed text base consists of "micro-structure" propositions. And these micro-structures together form a textual macro-structure.

Proposition serves as the interface of communication between lexical-grammatical meaning and textual meaning. It is a basic unit if we want to decompose comprehension process into components. (Kintsch & van Djik, 1978) It is assumed that the surface structure of a discourse consists of a set of ordered propositions, determined by various semantic relations among the propositions.

In addition to psychologists, functional and cognitive linguists are also interested in propositions and integrate propositions in their studies. Halliday (2010) considers that meaning is realized at three levels of discourse: phonological, lexical-grammatical and semantic levels. Propositions should fit in semantic level. Epistemic meaning defines proposition as "a meaning unit which can be said to have a truth value" (Kasper, 2012: 278). Epistemic meaning agrees with much of the literature in that a proposition is considered to be a linguistic prompt to evoke a process construed as referring, or relation.

To sum up, proposition is a key concept in semantic structure. It is useful not only in exploring textual meaning, but also in analyzing reproductive recall protocols. In this study, proposition is defined as a unit of information, combination of word concepts and relations and based upon lexicons in constituting meaning. The list of ordered propositions represents the meaning of a text. It is not only essential in textual production and comprehension, but also in meaning-based textual analysis and assessment. Propositions, in combination, could be used to analyze semantic information, both in the source text and the interpreted text.

3.1.2 The Evolution of Proposition: A Historical Approach

The history and development of the concept of proposition have been long and complex. In a non-philosophical sense, proposition is a mathematical term, inherent and timeless truth. The concept was introduced into the fields of philosophy and formal linguistics at the turn of the 19th and 20th century in order to study the relationship between language and meaning. (Gale, 1967; Crawford, 2008) These contemporary accounts of proposition derive as an opposition to subjectivism and idealism and British empiricism. (Crawford, 2008) The core of these accounts is that propositions are mind-independent, extra-linguistic abstract entities akin to those mathematical symbols. Ryle (2002) points out the necessity of introducing the concept of proposition lies in the co-effects of two closely related theoretical assumptions: ① the theory of the intentionality of consciousness, requiring that every mental act be directed towards some object; ② the theory of meaning as naming, the meaning of an expression being the object named by it. In this sense, proposition is an abstract object that serves as both the intentional object of a mental act and the meaning of the sentence formulating this act. The abstract nature of propositions could be found in Russel's definition that "we can make sure of some meaning for the word 'proposition' by saying that ... it shall mean the class of all sentences having the same significance as a given sentence" (1919: 208-209). To put it in another way, propositions are the meanings of what the writer/speaker wants to deliver in heart, yet he/she can have different propositional attitudes toward the same proposition at the same times, and several people can have different propositional attitudes toward the same proposition at the same and at the different times. Propositions are actually a neutral existence among these different propositional attitudes.

An early central topic around this issue is the role of propositions in connecting meaning and language. Frege (1918; cited in Crawford, 2008) makes some distinctions among: ① The sentence that is written or uttered; ② the mental ideas that it directly represents; ③ the proposition/thought that the sentence is intended to represent. He uses a mechanism of true-false to judge propositions. Every sentence, he assumes, has a reference or denotation. Reference refers to meaning or sense in language itself (truth-false), and denotation refers to contextual meaning. Wu (2007) further elaborates the differences among utterance, sentence and proposition. Utterances are "real pieces of speech" (2007: 40). A sentence is sure to be an utterance but an utterance not surely a sentence.

A proposition is a basic unit of sentential meaning, that is, a proposition is sure to be a sentence, but a sentence may contain several propositions. In other words, Utterances entail sentences, and sentences entail propositions.

Bealer (1998) proposes that each proposition is assigned a truth value; each property is assigned a set of items in the domain; each binary relation is assigned a set of ordered pairs of items in the domain. "The propositions which are true relative to it are the propositions which are actually true." (1998: 11), meaning that propositions are not truth value to possible worlds or entities, but are truth value to worlds or entities that are true to the speaker/writer.

Although philosophers such as Russel, Frege, Church and Carnap hold different notions of propositions and debate over the issues like "what propositions are" and "what natures they possess", they seem to consent to three major functions of propositions. Propositions are the linguistic meaning of the sentences, the contents of our sayings and thoughts. Meanwhile, they are the primary bearers of truth and falsity, playing a logical and judgmental role. Propositions are also the primary bearers of modal properties and logical relations.

These philosophical discussions of propositions mark a beginning of proposition-focused study in linguistics. They successfully define the nature of propositions in language and bridge over meaning and its linguistic representation. All these lay a theoretical foundation for future progress in semantics. However, some problems remain unsolved. First, the intentionality of proposition, as a major assumption, lacks a convincing explanation in formal linguistics. "I am hungry", spoken by two different persons, may represent different propositions and mental acts. This issue had been left for psycholinguists and cognitive linguists that would emerge since the 1960s. Second, for Frege's "true-false" judgment, he seems to miss possible criterion to carry it out, which makes it extremely hard to evaluate truth value or false value of a proposition.

With the development of psychology and cognitive studies in the 1960s, proposition theory found itself useful in investigating meaning construction and comprehension process. Fillmore (1968, 1969, 1971) was the first few to research proposition in this field. He classifies the types of lexical information to analyze "semantic properties" of speech acts, of which verbs serve an elementary function. He further analyzes the predicate structure, case structure and surface realization of arguments of lexicons. A major contribution is his proposal of verbal sub-classification. The classification is based on case theory, a theory of defining role structure of given expressions. He categorizes verb types into Agent (A), Counter-Agent (C), Object (O), Result (R), Instrument (I), Source (S), Goal (G) and Experiencer (E) (see Table 3.5):

Table 3.5 Verbal Types of Proposition (After Fillmore, 1971: 136)

Verb types	Description
Agent (A)	the instigator of the event
Counter-Agent (C)	the force or resistance against the action is carried out
Object (O)	the entity that moves or changes or whose position or existence is in consideration
Result (R)	the entity that comes into existence as a result of the action
Instrument (I)	the stimulus or immediate physical cause of an event
Source (S)	the place from which something moves
Goal (G)	the place to which something moves
Experiencer (E)	the entity which receives or accepts or experiences or undergoes the effect of an action

Fillmore paves the way for future development and orients further development of lexical-semantic theories. His "verbal types" directly results in propositional analysis of Turner and Greene (1977). However, Fillmore's classification of predicate and arguments is still largely based on traditional grammar, something that Kintsch and Lakeoff would try to detach from.

Kintsch (1974) discusses proposition in a systematic way. In Kintsch's eyes, proposition is not only suitable for linguistic studies, but also promising in psychological development. On the basis of Fillmore's theory of lexical types, Kintsch firstly proposes a hierarchy of meaning construction, including word concepts, proposition, text base and macrostructure, from bottom to top. These parts constitute structure of semantic memory and comprehension. Following the trail of Fillmore, Kintsch further elaborates on the classification of predicators and noun categories, and extends propositional analysis to metaphors. More constructively, Kinstch establishes a psychological process model that is intended to provide a framework for understanding how human intellectual works. Kintsch explains that people produce texts or discourse coherently because "the units of the system are not diffuse associations, but specific relations among them" (1974:42). With the experiments based on this model, Kintsch demonstrates how propositions represent the psychological reality. His psychological process model assumes that PA is capable of depicting psychological process. This assumption largely extends the application of PA, which later finds its use in assessing recall protocols.

Turner & Greene (1977) are among the few who study the construction and use of propositional analysis in textual analysis in the first place. They discuss the ordering of propositions in text base (a concept of textual structure), namely macrostructure. A step-by-step construction of a text base is provided to guide further application. A constructive contribution of this paper is that Turner & Greene apply PA to scoring recall protocols, with the assumption that complex linguistic materials can be reduced to a list of connected ideas, thus capable of being used to compare with the original texts. They claim that PA could simplify the task of scoring, while in the meantime ensure its reliability. The rationale underlying PA-based scoring criterion is that all propositions of a text base are listed out. The ones in recall protocols are compared with those in the source text, and then the percentage of acceptable correspondence is the score. While investigating the feasibility of PA in scoring recall protocols, the researchers raise the issue of rater leniency and severity. But they fail to offer solution to it.

On the other hand, there is no clear distinction of true and false correspondence, leaving it at raters' disposal. It seems that PA is a good proposal of scoring, but it is rather implausible because of lacking workable or feasible criterion.

A central issue of propositional theory has been truth conditions of meaning. If propositions are representations of mental thoughts, how could we judge whether they actually represent our thoughts? Or to what extent do propositions represent our thoughts? For the judgment of truth or false value of meaning, there are two pairs of concepts. The first pair is actual world and possible worlds. The way things exist is the actual world; the hypothetical ways that reality might be or might have been are possible worlds. The actual world is a part of possible worlds, as it is a possible reality. For the second pair, extension and intension, things that are referred to in actual worlds and possible worlds are regarded as extension and intension of words. Frege (1918) points out that the key to judging truth or false value of propositions lies in telling whether propositional extension is in line with the propositional intension. Kearns (2011) connects propositions with the actual world. To find out whether a sentence is true or false depends on whether the meaning of the sentence matches the way reality is:

> If you know the relevant facts about reality and you know what a sentence means, then you know whether it is true or false. If you know what a sentence means and you know that it is true, then you know the relevant facts. If you know a certain fact, and you know that the truth of a particular true sentence depends precisely on this fact, then you know what that sentence means. (Kearns, 2011: 8)

These theoretical discussions lay the foundation to put meaning-based value judgment of correspondence in translation and interpreting studies.

3.1.3 Propositional Correspondence Relations and Value Judgment

To tell the extent of correspondence between sentences, Kearns summarizes several important properties of statements in formal semantics: presupposition, entailment, contradiction and tautology. These properties underlie the logic of truth-based relations between sentences.

Presupposition is firstly proposed in formal semantics by Strawson (1950), in an effort to handle the difficulty of judging some sentences as being true or false. In the truth or false judgment of "The King of France is bald", it is hard to make the decision as there is no such person as the King of France. Strawson proposes that the use of an expression *the King of France* itself presupposes the existence of its referent, meaning that the presupposition of a sentence must be satisfied for the statement to have a truth value. If *the King of France* does not exist, we cannot tell the truth value of the sentence "The King of France is bald". It could be either true or false. The relationship of statement *A* and statement *B* is like:

① Statement *A* presupposes *B*.

② If *A* is true, then *B* is true.

③ If *A* is false, then *B* is neither true nor false.

④ If *B* is false, then *A* is true.

⑤ If *not-B* is true, then *A* is true.

In Example ③, *B* is always true, regardless of the situations "*A is false*" or "*not-A is true*". Kearns calls it "presupposition survives negation". For example:

a. John no longer writes fictions.

b. John is still writing fictions.

These two statements have the same presupposition: John once wrote fictions. No matter whether John is writing fictions or John no longer writes fictions, it is assumed that John once wrote fictions. Then, "John once wrote fictions" presupposes "John no longer writes fictions" and "John is still writing fictions".

Another relation, entailment, could also be described with computing logics. A statement *A* entails a statement *B* if wherever *A* is true, *B* must also be true. When *B* is not true, *A* cannot be true. The full pattern is shown below:

① Statement *A* presupposes *B*.

② If *A* is true, *B* is true.

③ If *B* is not true, *A* is not true.

④ If *A* is not true, *B* is either true or false.

Let us see some examples:

a. *The window is open* entails *The window is not closed.*

b. *Sam is shorter than John* entails *John is taller than Sam.*

The difference between presupposition and entailment is that presupposition survives negation while entailment could not. Presupposition is about the existence or presence of a predicate, usually a "there-be" concern. Entailment is an "Yes" or "No" issue. Please see following examples:

a. *The King of France is bald* entails *There is a King of France.*

b. *The King of France is not bald* entails *There is a King of France.*

c. *Hunt is a bulldog* entails *Hunt is a dog.*

d. *Hunt is not a bulldog* does not entail *Hunt is a dog.*

A clear demarcation of presupposition and entailment is given by Kearns (2011:19): "Presupposition is a special kind of entailment, specifically one that is not cancelled by negating the statement which carries it—presupposition survives negation. Because presupposition is a kind of entailment, it is part of the literal sense of the statement which carries the presupposition. A presupposition attaches to a statement or sentence according to its literal meaning and doesn't depend on a particular context."

Despite its independence of context, presupposition cannot be said to be context-free. Jaszczolt (2002) mentions that presupposition is pragmatically related to some degree. In a conversation, statements may often carry presuppositions that the hearer doesn't know to be true, but doesn't object to, as well. Hearers may accommodates these presuppositions by simply accepting them as facts. For example:

"It is quite a good supermarket. When I came in with my wife and my son, we soon got what each of us had wanted."

This utterance entails that *I have wife and son*, and in a wider context that *they shopped in the supermarket once*. The hearer is easily accommodating this presupposition. This is called presupposition accommodation.

For the third type of relationship, contradiction, it means that statement *A* and statement *B* could not be both true under any circumstances. If the contradictory statements *A* and *B* are together in a complex statement *C*, *C* is also called a contradiction. See the following examples:

a. *Richard is out* contradicts *Richard is at home*, and vice versa.

b. *He runs fast and slowly* is a contradiction.

A contradiction can never be true because either *A* or *B* can be true. However, a tautology is a statement that is true all the time. For example:

a. *When we eat, teeth will move.*

b. *The white wall uses white paint.*

Entailment and presupposition are the two most important and frequently used in semantic analysis. Linguists who are interested in meaning equivalence in propositions are likely to use these logical relations as tools for analysis. With the further penetration of semantics and pragmatics in IS, together with an urgent need of meaning-based assessment in IS, scholars are turning their eyes to this instrument, exploring feasibility and applicability of propositional analysis in IS. This is to be presented in detail in the following section.

3.2 PA in Interpreting Studies[1]

With the development of semantics and interpreting studies, there is an increasing call for interdisciplinary studies of these two fields. As IS is essentially focused on sense/meaning, propositional analysis meets such demand, playing an instrumental role in textual and information processing analysis. Propositional analysis in IS is used mainly in two approaches: as a major target of research or as an instrument of research. The first approach is to study propositions directly in IS; the second approach is to use proposition indirectly, as a tool of research.

3.2.1 Proposition as a Major Target in IS

In the 1980s, researchers made first attempt in discussion of potential use of PA in IS. Mackintosh (1985) makes one of the earliest attempts to introduce PA into IS. As a response to Gerver's information processing model in interpreting, she refutes that the model, stressing the phonological input and memory segments, fails to explain information processing in a semantic way. She raises questions as to the identification and reproduction of meaning. During the course of seeking answers, she adopts the Kintsch and van Djik's PA Model, concerning macro-structure and micro-propositions. Linking this model to conference interpreters' performance, Mackintosh claims that the model offers a theoretical description of the comprehension and production processes and PA provides possible explanations for interpreting errors and omissions. The study, for the first time, testifies the applicability of PA in IS theoretically.

---

[1] Propositional analysis is text-based. The rationale and methods of PA in interpreting studies are in the same way as those in translation studies, and PA in interpreting studies outnumbers that in translation studies. As the present study mainly discusses interpreter performance tests, application of PA in translation studies is not involved.

Isham & Lane (1993) practically confirm that information processing and production are based on propositions, or units of meaning. They conclude that interpreters, similar to listeners, process sentences with lexical substitution or syntactical restructuring, based on the purpose of representing propositions, rather than representing the form of the sentences themselves. This study proves that information is processed at propositional, or semantic level, rather than lexical or syntactical level.

Padilla, Bajo & Padilla (1998) share a similar perception by considering propositions as units of meaning representation. They adopt a constructive view of information processing, regarding comprehension as a constructive, not serial process, and that the mediator constructs a mental model of communication. Furthermore, they construct a model of mental representation in translation and interpreting, containing various levels such as phonological and orthographic level, lexical-semantic level, propositional level, micro-structure level and macro-structural level. However, they don't take proposition as a unit of performance assessment. In terms of error classification, they just consider "a combination of the analysis of errors in the three tasks of mediation, with an analysis of think-aloud protocols ...regarding global processes such as comprehension" (1998:74). Their standards for error classification are vague and ambiguous.

These studies represent initial attempts to introduce propositional analysis into IS and verify its feasibility and applicability in IS theoretically, paving the way for further practical investigation of PA in IS. But there is a serious drawback that cannot be ignored—these studies take propositions as units of meaning representation, without defining propositions clearly and properly. What they depend upon is Kintsch's psychological and cognitive perception of propositions. But without a clear statement of propositional analysis frame in interpreting, it is difficult to understand how to put PA in practice. It is undeniable that PA is just a term borrowed from psychological field and semantics, hardly integrated into IS. There is a demand to adapt propositions to the characteristics of interpreting, and to set up a clear criterion so that PA could fit the needs of IS and be truly a tool for information assessment.

3.2.2 PA as a Research Instrument in IS

In addition to the previous studies of targeting propositions, there are multi-dimensional studies which use PA as a research instrument. These studies employ PA as a means for sense/meaning analysis. The reason for the prevailing application of PA is that propositions, as units of meaning free from lexical concerns, are perfect units for investigating information processing in interpreting.

From a cognitive perspective, Lambert (1998) bases his research on PA to investigate the differences of information processing among listening, shadowing and simultaneous interpreting. Similarly, Dillinger (1989, 1994) employs PA to compare comprehension in simultaneous interpreting and comprehension in non-interpreting situations.

Lemieux & Hamers (1995), from a neuroscience perspective, investigate how earedness in SI influences the functions of our brain hemispheres. Tommola, et al. (2000), Rinne (2000) and Hamers, et al. (2002) make use of MRI to explore how SI, paraphrasing and directionality would have impacts on brain activity and hemisphere preference. These studies also use propositions as research tools.

Sunnari (1995) studies differences in strategies between expert and novice interpreters. Sunnari concludes that experts are more apt to segment information into propositions, implying that experts differ from novice in that they prefer to proposition-based information processing and production, a skill that the novice are not that capable.

These researchers base their studies on propositions or propositional analysis. Taking propositions as units of meaning, they can focus on how information/ meaning is processed and how meaning is construed and represented in language, avoiding falling into the unwanted trap of lexical equivalence. These studies, however, face the criticism similar to those studies in the previous section—lacking clarified criterion for PA. All these studies clearly state that they examine proposition-based information, but none illustrates how they do so, and what criterion they follow.

3.2.3 Current Development of PA in IS

The past decades has witnessed the development of PA in psychological science and its use in IS. Its applications in neuroscience and cognitive science have proved PA to be a useful instrument in detecting information processing and meaning reformulation. (Lemieux & Hamers, 1995; Hamers, etc. 2002) These findings facilitate the use of PA in IS, where researchers are in search of such a tool to analyze interpreting performance, either in professional or educational contexts.

Offering a unit of meaning representation, PA fits in IS naturally, especially in terms of the assessment of information fidelity. It has been discovered that PA is applicable and instrumental in analyzing information equivalence between the source and target texts. (Sunnari, 1995; Tommola & Helevä, 1998) Therefore, PA, when combined with modern technology and psychometric measures, could serve as a powerful tool in IS and QI assessment, in which information fidelity is regarded as a key construct.

In view of its significance in IS, PA is still under-developed, currently. Firstly, PA in IS centers around its theoretical establishment and applicability. Scholars interested in PA tend to turn a blind eye to the standardized procedure of PA when drawing reference from semantics. In other words, researchers apply the concept of proposition and use it to analyze information in interpreting product, stating that their research is PA-based. However, they fail to mention the identification and classification procedure of propositions, as could be seen from the literature (Tommola, et al. 1995, 1998, 2000; Sunnaris, 1998). Provided that, researchers borrow the concept of proposition, but fail to adopt PA.

Secondly, PA in IS lacks clearly defined criteria in the assessment of information fidelity. The theory of proposition does include not only discourse propositionalization, but also its unique rules of propositional analysis. When proposition is gaining popularity in IS, the call for clearer and fine-grained standard of PA grows.

Generally speaking, in the wake of preliminary stage of applying PA to IS, it is high time to further integrate PA into IS, establishing standardized PA identification and classification procedure to ensure validity of PA-based research. In the mean time, it is significant to expand and enrich the potential use of PA in IS, such as QI assessment in educational contexts and explore its implications for interpreter education.

3.3 Analytical Framework for the PA-Based Assessment of Information Fidelity in Consecutive Interpreting

3.3.1 Coding Scheme of PA

The previous section concludes with some existing problems of PA in IS. A prominent problem is that PA lacks standardized criteria and methods of operation. This problem has drawn attention of some linguists and interpreting researchers.

Tommola and his partners (1995, 1998, 2000) have been the few who design a relatively applicable propositional scoring technique to measure information fidelity in interpreting. In his experiments, he employs PA to examine the effects of language directionality and text complexity on trainee performance in simultaneous interpreting. Besides, they specifically propose and testify a feasible proposition analytic scheme, which exemplifies the feasibility of PA in IS. Despite these achievements, their analytical scheme is rough on sub-categories for the classification of propositional accuracy in terms of the source and target discourse, which is hard to replicate and disseminate for other researchers.

Since Church's proposal of comparing propositions in the source and translated texts, researchers have made great efforts in this trail, especially in integrating PA into translation and interpreting studies. However, scholars always concentrate on the conceptual issues of propositions and ignore the instrumental part of propositions—logical relations/properties. In previous sections, these logical relations of propositions are illustrated, which language philosophers and semanticists develop and use for detecting equivalence in meaning. One possible reason for this negligence is that logical relations, developed in line with formal linguistics, are considered to be unsuitable for cognitive and psychological investigation of texts or utterance. Another reason is perhaps related to the complexity nature of interpreting itself. Pöchhacker(2001) questions that these scorable textual parameters (error counts, propositional accuracy scores, etc.) cover only certain aspects of quality, which are unlikely to reflect gross adequacy or quality, as there are other critical parameters such as voice, idiomaticity, context, etc. But when it comes to the topic of interpreting assessment which requires an objective, standardized and feasible criterion, the seemingly formal style of PA makes sense. The doubt could further be mitigated when most influential interpreter performance tests are embracing componential assessment sheets, assessing critical competence of interpreters respectively, with information fidelity accounting for a major component.

Yeh (2015) tries to apply conceptual and assessing components of PA to interpreting assessment. Firstly, Yeh insists that propositions should be units of meaning representation in interpreting assessment. The propositionalization process is based on Bovair and Kieras' method (1985), constructing propositions with predicates and arguments. Then, by Barik's error categories, he tells that errors in interpreting include omission, addition and substitution. Yeh further sub-classifies interpreting errors, on the basis of logical relations of propositions, into entailment, presupposition and contradiction. See the Table 3.6 below Yeh's whole correspondence scheme:

Table 3.6 Propositional Correspondence Scheme (Adapted from Yeh, 2015: 22)

Match		
No.	Code	Full Description
1	M	Complete Match
2	M-PREED	Match-Meaning Presupposed
3	M-ENTED	Match-Meaning Entailed
4	O-PSVING	Omission-Meaning Preserving
Misinterpreting		
No.	Code	Full Description
1	M-U-PREING	Match-Unclear-Meaning Presupposing
2	M-U-ENTING	Match-Unclear-Meaning Entailing
3	M-ALTED	Match-Meaning Altered
4	O	Omission
Corresponding		
No.	Code	Full Description
1	M	Match
2	A-PSVING	Addition-Meaning Preserving
3	M-PREED	Match-Meaning Presupposed
4	M-ENTED	Match-Meaning Entailed
Disinterpreting		
No.	Code	Full Description
1	M-U-PREING	Match-Unclear-Meaning Presupposing
2	M-U-ENTING	Match-Unclear-Meaning Entailing
3	M-ALTING	Match-Meaning Altering
4	A-ALTING	Addition-Meaning Altering

In the scheme, Yeh defines propositional correspondence into four categories: Match, Misinterpreting, Correspondence, and Disinterpreting. Category "Match" refers to a situation where two propositions could match in form and meaning in both languages. Misinterpreting refers to a situation where propositions do not match at lexical levels, and are unclear in meaning. Correspondence refers to a situation where propositions do not match at lexical levels, but match semantically. Disinterpreting refers to a situation where propositions could match lexically, but it is unclear whether meaning is corresponding or not.

Yeh further explains that these categories and sub-sets are related, and even some sub-sets are defined from the angel of source discourse or interpreted discourse, seeing the details in Table 3.7:

Table 3.7 Propositional Correspondence Scheme for the Source Text and
the Interpreted Text (Adapted from Yeh, 2015: 23)

Interpreted		Source	
A-PSVING	Corresponding		
M	Corresponding	Match	M
M-ENTED	Corresponding	Misinterpreting	M-U-ENTING
M-PREED	Corresponding	Misinterpreting	M-U-PREING
M-U-ENTING	Disinterpreting	Match	M-ENTED
M-U-PREING	Disinterpreting	Match	M-PREED
M-ALTING	Disinterpreting	Misinterpreting	M-ALTED
A-ALTING	Disinterpreting		
		Misinterpreting	Omission

With these logical relations, Yeh claims that by calculating the propositions that preserve the original meaning, researchers can give a score for interpreting text. In his experiment, inter-rater reliability reaches 0.957, a value that achieves statistical significance, which means that this coding scheme is acceptable and operable among raters.

Yeh's study is the first attempt to consider logical relations of propositions in IS. Data prove that this scheme is reliable and operable among raters. This coding scheme gets away with traditional approaches of PA at lexical levels, and standardizes operation processes, leaving behind rater subjectivity to some degree.

Of course, Yeh's coding scheme is not without its problems. Firstly, the scheme is bi-dimensional in that it considers propositional correspondence from the source and interpreted texts respectively. On the basis of this bi-dimensionality, Yeh gets two fidelity scores, the first score comes from assessment when taking source text as reference, and the second score comes from the assessment when taking the interpreted text as reference. Here comes the problem: raters will feel confused with the rating scale and the logical relations. For instance, the relation M-ENTED for the interpreted text corresponds to M-U-ENTING for the source text. This mixed criterion is not clarified for raters. Secondly, Yeh validates this scheme by means of inter-rater reliability alone. These drawbacks, if taken without care, are likely to encounter doubts and criticism.

Insofar, proposition, being a unit of meaning representation in language, has found its use in interpreting assessment. It is believed that propositional analysis will supply alternative insights for interpreting performance assessment. Furthermore, it can offer valid evidence in revealing trainees' flaws, a clue that inspires trainers and trainees to better improve holistic training process. Based on previous discussions of development of interpreting assessment studies, especially latest progress in the assessment of information fidelity, together with recent breakthrough in propositional analysis, the author then proposes an analytical framework (Figure 3.2) for the present investigation.

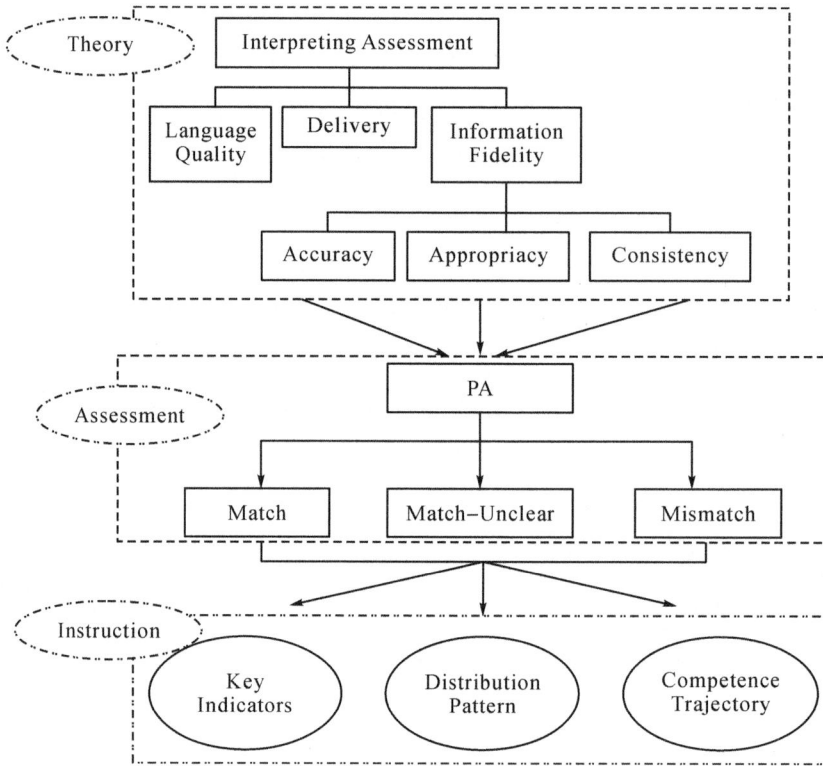

Figure 3.2 Analytical Framework for the PA-Based Assessment of Information Fidelity in Consecutive Interpreting

3.3.2 Analytical Framework for the PA-Based Assessment of Information Fidelity in Consecutive Interpreting

At present, interpreting assessment lends itself to subjective assessment and calls for quantified and relatively objective assessment. There are three major criteria in assessment: information fidelity, delivery and target language quality (Lee, 2008; Lee, 2015; Han, 2015). With information fidelity being the most important construct of all, it attracts lots of attention as well. Information fidelity can be assessed from three perspectives: accuracy, appropriacy and consistency. (Cai, 2006) All these perspectives could be represented and assessed by means of PA. That is, information accuracy is represented by word concepts; appropriacy represented by mood and modality, as proposition will take into account word concepts that represent feelings and emotions; and consistency represented by pronouns and logical relations. In such sense, proposition, containing all the three aspects of fidelity evaluation, can serve as a basic information assessment unit. In addition, semantics has developed a set of linguistic markers and computational methods, as an interface between meaning and linguistic representations. The computational method in semantics could provide assessment a tool that is capable of quantifying and specifying linguistic markers, eliminating the much-criticized subjectivity and personal bias.

Adapted from Yeh's propositional correspondence scheme, PA in this study takes propositions in the source texts as reference (see Table 3.6). Accordingly, propositional correspondence is simplified to three categories: Match, Match-Unclear and Mismatch. The classification is different from Yeh's in that it cuts out some types, which appear in situations where interpreted text is considered as reference. As a matter of fact, during QI rating process, source text is considered as reference. Category "match" includes three types of propositional correspondence: Match, Match-Meaning Entailed, Match-Meaning Presupposed. Category Match-Unclear includes Match-Meaning Unclear-Entailed, Match-Unclear-Meaning Presupposed and Match-Meaning Altered. Mismatch includes Addition-Meaning Preserved, Addition-Meaning Altered and Omission. The coding scheme of propositional correspondence in this study is shown in Table 3.8 below:

Table 3.8 Coding Scheme of PA in the Present Study

Match		
No.	Code	Explanation
1	M	Complete Match
2	M-PREED	Match-Meaning Presupposed
3	M-ENTED	Match-Meaning Entailed

Continued

Match-Unclear		
No.	Code	Explanation
1	M-U-PREED	Match-Unclear-Meaning Presupposed
2	M-U-ENTED	Match-Unclear-Meaning Entailed
3	M-ALTED	Match-Meaning Altered
Mismatch		
No.	Code	Explanation
1	A-PSVED	Addition-Meaning Preserved
2	A-ALTED	Addition-Meaning Altered
3	O	Omission

This classification of propositional correspondence of interpreted texts against source texts offers fresh insights for interpreting assessment, being an alternative to traditional assessment instrument, which largely depends on raters' personal experience and expertise. Even more, this proposition-based assessment offers a new tool for quantifiable and operable assessment, with potential for applications in computed-based assessment. It is supposed to be capable of mitigating subjectivity in the assessment of information fidelity of interpreting performance, and consequently enable scores to better mirror examinees' competence in message transfer, free from rater's personal bias. The identification and classification procedure of the coding scheme in interpreting performance test is described in Section 4.2.

From a pedagogical perspective, data extracted from PA could reveal much hidden information of examinees. By examining the relationship between fidelity scores and frequencies of various types of propositional correspondence, it is possible to figure out key indicators that reveal examinees' competence in message transfer. By comparing the distribution patterns of propositional correspondence between high-score examinees and low-score examinees, it is convenient to tell on what aspects that instructors could focus and provide customized instructions. All these could offer exciting insights and inspirations to interpreter instructors.

With the theoretical and analytical framework of PA in the assessment of information fidelity being established, it is time to validate it in interpreting performance tests. Validation of PA as an assessment tool will be achieved with an experiment of over 40 participants. Meanwhile, the PA-based assessment criterion will be validated from the perspectives of its construct validity, criterion validity and rating validity, by means of comparing data from the PA-based criterion with those from a current in-use criterion. Detailed experiment and analysis procedures are described in the next chapter.

3.4 Summary

This chapter has proposed an analytical framework on which empirical investigation in later chapters is based. To this end, the concept of proposition is elaborated and further operationalized by drawing on inquiries into previous discussions over interpreting assessment studies, especially studies on the assessment of information fidelity. The theoretical discussions of PA in interpreting studies allow a thorough understanding of its potential use in the assessment of interpreting quality and interpreter training.

Moreover, the experimental study of PA in interpreting assessment is brought to notice as part of its empirical feasibility, on which the study is based and pushed forward towards this direction. Numerous researchers have adopted the concept of proposition as linguistic representation of meaning, including some in the field of translation and interpreting studies. Proposition has been a basic unit of meaning in both translation and interpreting. Of course, we also need to be aware that the view of proposition as a meaning unit itself, rather than what it really embodies or represents, constrains a further application of it in related areas.

In the analytical framework, the assessment of information fidelity is divided into categories, which then are further specified into semantic markers. This framework forms an interface of theoretical components of the assessment criterion and semantic representation of meaning in language. Propositions, as meaning units of language, serve as the bridge.

All interpreting studies will wind a way to interpreter training. After all, training is the core of interpreting studies. (Pöchhacker, 2016) The test use covers a wide spectrum. Training, as one possible test use, is frequently sought after but rarely touched upon in this aspect. Instructors and test designers may have a good will in applying test results to classroom teaching, but feel invalid without proper methodological and statistical means. PA, with concrete data in information fidelity, could help inspire instructors to analyze interpreter performance in certain aspect and to revise their teaching syllabus accordingly, which helps establish proper communication between testing and teaching.

Chapter 4

The Experiment

Following a brief review of propositional studies that lay theoretical and analytical foundation for the empirical study of the assessment of information fidelity, this chapter will present the experimental methodology to validate the PA-based assessment in interpreting, including components of its design, such as objectives, subjects, materials, data collection, and scoring criteria.

4.1 Objectives

To examine the proposed theoretical and analytical framework, an experiment is designed and conducted in interpreting training context to validate PA in interpreting assessment on the one hand, and its implications for interpreter education on the other hand. The experiment is intended to find out whether scoring results of the proposed PA correlate to a mainstream rater/expert assessment criterion. And if so, to what extent the hypothesized PA assessment is reliable.

Considering proposition as a basic information assessment unit, the experiment also attempts to investigate the advantages and disadvantages of PA approach in the assessment of information fidelity in comparison with an in-use assessment criterion. In the next chapter, the investigation steps further as to make use of the PA-extracted data to explore its potential use in interpreter education.

4.2 Subjects

4.2.1 Test Participants

A number of 44 first-year students from four universities participate in the study. All these students are in MTI (Master of Translation and Interpreting) programs.

Demographically, in the subject group, there are 32 female students and 12 male students, aging from 20—25, with a mean age of 22.7.

As far as their learning experience and working experience are concerned, 20 out of the 44 participants graduated from Bachelor of Translation and Interpreting (BTI) programs, who have studied interpreting for more than two and a half years. The remaining 24 are English majors with an average of one and a half years of learning experience of interpreting. 8 participants have passed the exam CATTI (Level 3); 2 have passed the exam of CATTI (Level 2); 11 participants passed the exam of Shanghai Certificates of Interpreters (Advanced Level or Intermediate Level).

As to their working experience, 39 participants, accounting for nearly 90% of the total participants, have zero hour working experience. The rest 5 participants have been part-time or makeshift interpreters, with their working hours ranging from 5—30 hours. Offers have been mostly provided by teachers, or translation agencies.

At the time of the experiment, the participants have been attending consecutive interpreting courses for around a year during MTI study.

4.2.2 Raters

The author hires 3 raters to assess interpreting test materials. Raters are all PhD candidates in interpreting studies, with an average of 6 years of relevant teaching experience. All of them have received professional training of interpreting or attended interpreting-related courses. They have been interpreting raters (certification tests or contests) and received proper rating training previously. Raters' demographic information is shown in Table 4.1.

Table 4.1 Raters' Demographic Information

Rater	Gender	Interpreting Exp. (hours)	Rating Exp. (Yes/No)
1	Male	120	Y
2	Male	80	Y
3	Female	150	Y

4.3 Materials

4.3.1 Test Materials

Audio materials of the experiments are adapted from an English speech in the English Interpreting Certificate Test of Xiamen University (EIC Level 3). The topic of the speech is Small and Medium-sized Enterprises (SMEs) and Mobile Technologies. The total speech lasts for 6 minutes 53 seconds, with 830 words.

The text difficulty and complexity are examined by online text analysis tool Coh-Metrix, developed by Graesser and McNamara (http://cohmetrix. com/). Table 4.2 illustrates some key parameters of the test speech analyzed by Coh-Metrix. Lexical diversity is one of the key parameters of textual difficulty. (Huang & Bao, 2016) Normally, the higher the type-token ratio (TTR), the more difficult the text is. The TTR of the test speech is 0.6, which falls exactly into the generic TTR of science and tech category. (Yu & Xiao, 2018) The speech is about mobile technology and economy, which means that the speech fits the linguistic features of sci-tech text. The Flesch reading ease index, which is also frequently used to investigate the text difficulty, is 48.2, deemed appropriate for college-level readers (Kinkaid et al., 1975). Furthermore, terminology and topic are offered a week ahead for the examinees to prepare for background and topical knowledge.

Table 4.2 Difficulty Parameters of the Speech by Coh-Metrix

Number Label	Label V2.x	Text	Full Description
			Descriptive
1 DESPC	READNP	13	Paragraph count, number of paragraphs
2 DESSC	READNS	50	Sentence count, number of sentences
3 DESWC	READNW	830	Word count, number of words
4 DESPL	READAPL	3.846	Paragraph length, number of sentences in a paragraph, mean
5 DESPLd	n/a	2.035	Paragraph length, number of sentences in a paragraph, standard deviation
6 DESSL	READASL	16.600	Paragraph length, number of words, mean
7 DESSLd	n/a	9.998	Paragraph length, number of words, standard deviation
8 DESWLsy	READASW	1.675	Word length, number of syllables, mean
9 DESWLsyd	n/a	0.980	Word length, number of syllables, standard deviation
10 DESWLlt	n/a	5.006	Word length, number of letters, mean
11 DESWLltd	n/a	2.766	Word length, number of letters, standard deviation
			Lexical Diversity
12 LDTTRc	TYPTOKc	0.604	Lexical diversity, type-token ratio, content word lemmas
13 LDTTRa	n/a	0.440	Lexical diversity, type-token ratio, all words
14 LDMTLD	LEXDIVTD	86.217	Lexical diversity, MTLD, all words
15 LDVOCD	LEXDIVVD	98.437	Lexical diversity, VOCD, all words
			Readability
16 RDFRE	READFRE	48.281	Flesch reading ease
17 RDFKGL	READFKGL	10.649	Flesch-Kincaid grade level
18 RDL2	L2	10.686	Coh-Metrix L2 readability

At the beginning of the test, test directions and situations are read to the participants, so that they could be stimulated into the context. The test situation is read as "An analyst from an American research institute speaks to a group of leaders from small and medium-sized enterprises (SMEs) about mobile technologies and their impact on the economy, their industry and on SMEs".

The audio clip is separated into seven segments. At the end of each part, there will be an interval pause, and a sound signal to notify participants to start interpreting, and also a sound to signify the end of interpreting. The length of each pause is determined by the length of the speech part, about 1.3 times longer than the speech part. Words of the segments range from 82 to 140 and a weighted score is assigned to each segment in terms of information fidelity in the assessment sheet.

This English speech is read by a native speaker. The mean delivery rate is 120 words per minute, which falls within normal speech rate range of English speakers (cf. Huang & Bao, 2016).

Using test materials from the English Interpreting Certificate Test of Xiamen University is largely because of its assurance of test authenticity and delicate design. Initiated in 2002, EIC is a test organized and sponsored by Xiamen University Accreditation Centre for Interpreters and Translators. Boasting of a faculty of experienced interpreters and instructors, the Centre has organized the test for 16 consecutive years. The test is designed and carried out under the guideline of authenticity and scientific design, foregrounding an authentic interpreting environment for test takers. (Chen, 2003) It is because of the authentic working environment that the test has gained fame and reputation at home and abroad.

4.3.2 Assessment Materials

There are two assessment criteria. The first criterion consists of a rating scale and an assessment sheet designed by EIC testing committee. Originally, there are two macro-criteria in consideration: information fidelity and professional performance (quality of target language, expression, coping tactics and professionalism). As this experiment is intended to investigate information fidelity, the author only adopts the first part. The rating scale concerning information fidelity is classified into 5 bands, taking into account the rate of message transfer, minor and major deviations and omissions. The total score of the information part is 30 points. A score is allocated to each of the seven segments respectively, based on the information density of each segment.

There are reasons for the choice of the EIC rating scale and assessment sheet as a criterion for the assessment of information fidelity in the present study. First, the EIC test materials, when combined with its assessment scale and sheet, could elicit authentic performance and extract data as a complete system. Second, the EIC assessment sheet assigns a weighted score to each segment on the basis of information density, which makes it possible for raters to score segmental information independently, free from "halo effect" of previous segments. Further, the weighted scores assigned to the segments enable raters to quantify and assess information fidelity based on examinees' performance, which makes it possible to be measured against the scores of the PA-based criterion. Fourth, other ATI performance tests deploy various assessment sheets, whether a holistic one or scale-based one. It is hard to find a widely-recognized assessment sheet. With those reasons considered, the EIC fidelity assessment scale and sheet are deemed appropriate and feasible in the current experiment (see Table 4.3).

Table 4.3 The EIC Fidelity Assessment Scale and Sheet

	Descriptors	Band
Information Fidelity	The original messages are nearly completely delivered (i. e., >95%), with few deviations, inaccuracies, and minor/major omissions.	5
	A substantial amount of original messages delivered (i. e., >80%), with a few number of deviations, inaccuracies, and minor/major omissions.	4

Continued

	Descriptors	Band
Information Fidelity	Majority of original messages delivered (i. e., 60%—70%), with a small number of deviations, inaccuracies, and minor/major omissions.	3
	Minority of original messages delivered (i.e.,40%—50%), with some instances of major deviations, inaccuracies and omissions.	2
	A small portion of original messages delivered (i. e., <30%), with frequent occurrences of deviations, inaccuracies, and minor/major omissions, to such a degree that listeners may doubt the integrity of renditions.	1

	Student	Score
Information Fidelity	S1 (5 points)	4
	S2 (4 points)	4
	S3 (5 points)	5
	S4 (5 points)	5
	S1 (5 points)	5
	S5 (5 points)	5
	S6 (3 points)	3
	S7 (3 points)	3

The second assessment material is not in the form of assessment sheet, but an Excel format file. Propositions of the source text and the target text are listed in the files. Raters will score the performance at the end of the file, according to the correspondence rate between propositions of the source text and the target text. In the meantime, types of correspondence will be labeled and counted at the end of each file (see Table 4.4).

Table 4.4 The PA-Based Information Fidelity Assessment Sheet

命题号	述语	论元一	论元二	类别	命题	论元	论述一	论述二
P01	and	ladies	gentlemen		P01		女士们	先生们
P02	good	morning			P02	好	大家	
P03		Previlege	I		P03	今天		
P04	SPEAK	P03	mobile technologies		P04	知道	我们	
					P05	不断发展	美国	中小型企业
P05	refer to	mobile	P06		P06	给	P05	我们的经济
P06		technologies	all		P07	带来	活力	非常大的
P07	enable	P06	P08		P08	促进	相关产业	发展
P08	and	voice services	data services					
P09	via	cellular connectivity			P09	很高兴	我	P09
P10	including	2G network			P10	开幕演讲	科技研讨会	
P11	including	3G network						
P12	including	4G network			P11	经历	我们	时代
					P12	大发展	通信工具	时代
P13	Rapid diffusion	mobile technologies			P13	包括	工具	2G
P14	in	P13	P16		P14			3G
P15	first	decade			P15			4G
P16	P15	new millenium			P16	扩散和传播	他们	不断
P17	has	P13	P19					
P18	Negate	precedent			P17	如今		
P19	has	P18	history		P18	不断发展	通信技术	全球
					P19	而	目前	
P20	Negate	technology	other		P20	带来	通信技术	市值
P21	Be	P20	hands of people		P21		市值	约3.3万亿美元
P22	Be	P20	countries		P22	波及	这些发展	24个国家
P23	Be	P20	short time		P23	创造	这些发展	11万工作岗位

4.4　Procedures

4.4.1　Experiment Process

Preparation: One week ahead of the test, the theme and key words are sent out to participants, so that they could prepare themselves with relevant background knowledge and technical terminology.

Equipment check: The test is held in multi-media classrooms. Each participant is equipped with headset and microphone. Equipments are tested beforehand and confirmed noise-proof, to make sure that the examinees will not be disturbed by sounds from others. Instructor's computer is the control center, which can record participants' sound and save in the PC in ".mp3" files.

Warm-up: Just before the interpreting test, an audio English speech will be played as warm-up listening. Examinees could check whether their headsets and microphones are working properly. Also, this warm-up listening could help them get into the working state. The speech is adapted from Speech of Apple CEO at the Commencement Ceremony of Duke University. The speech lasts for about 5 minutes. There is an interval pause at the end of each segment, with a signal noticing the start of interpreting and another signal noticing the end of interpreting. Instructor then replays the recordings to make sure that microphones and recorders are well functioning.

Test: The audio is played to the participants. Directions and situations are presented at the beginning. The speech consists of seven parts. There is a pause after the reading of every segment, with a sound signal to notify the beginning of the pause and another sound signal to notify the end of the pause. Participants could interpret during the intervals. They could take notes during the test. After the last pause, instructor will mark the end of the test. Then he collects the recordings and save them in ".mp3" format files.

Questionnaire: After the test, the instructor spreads out a questionnaire to the participants. The questionnaire contains 6 questions, centering on their self-perception of existing problems in this task and their expectations for future training. When they hand in the filled questionnaire, a present is given to each of them as a token of appreciation.

Sample processing: When all the 44 sample materials in ".mp3" format are collected, they are edited in the first place. Source text reading is removed from the audio files, with the use of software Adobe Audition, only subjects' interpreting performance remains. Then, the clean audio files are duplicated and grouped into two documents, one document for PA and one for EIC assessment.

Audio files in the PA document are then uploaded to IFly website (http://www.iflyrec.com/) for transcription. When all transcripts are collected, with each examinee's interpreting text in a ".txt" file, a manual check is conducted, so as to get rid of incorrect characters and mis-transcripts. After that, the clean transcripts are propopositionalized with software CPIDR and manual identification. At last, the propositions of each interpreted text are input into an "xls." file in alignment with propositions of the source speech.

Audio files in EIC document are clean audios. Also in the EIC document are the EIC information fidelity assessment sheets.

4.4.2 Rater Training

Rating process consists of two phases. In Phase 1, raters assess the propositionalized texts. Phase 2 takes place 3 weeks after Phase 1, so as to minimize the effects of Phase 1 rating on Phase 2 rating. Before each phase of rating, raters are invited to attend a rater training session.

Days before Phase 1 and Phase 2 training sessions, a background reading material pack covering the source speech and PA or EIC assessment sheets is sent to the raters by email, so that raters could familiarize the topic and get acquaintance with the assessment rules.

As shown in Table 4.5, to minimize practice effects, the raters are given sufficient time to warm up. To offset fatigue effects, interval short breaks are offered during the training session. The training session lasts about 2.5 hours.

Training of PA is the most important of the session, which consists of four steps. First, definition and key concepts of proposition are introduced. Raters could raise questions thereafter. When the raters are sure of understanding the concept, propositional correspondence relations are listed and explained. Examples are offered and explained. After that, the trainer introduces rules of identification and classification of proposition correspondence, followed by discussion and question-answering, until everything is clear.

The next part of the session is pilot assessment, which is carried out in two rounds. In the first round, 10 propositionalized sentences (5 English sentences and 5 corresponding interpreted Chinese sentences) are presented for the raters to assess. When it is finished, all the 3 raters explain their assessment. When there appear different ideas about propositional correspondence, discussion begins until doubts are settled. The second round is the assessment of 4 propositionalized paragraphs (2 English paragraphs and 2 corresponding interpreted Chinese paragraphs). The discussion goes on until the raters settle all differences. It should be noted that the raters and the trainer only discuss identification and classification of propositions, which do not involve rating scores.

Table 4.5 Phase 1: Rater Training Procedure

1. Warm-up (ethics clearance, rapport-building)
2. Rating introduction, followed by a 5-minute break
2.1. Rating materials
2.2. Assessment procedure
3. Propositional analysis, followed by a 15-minute break
3.1. Basic concept of proposition
3.2. Semantic relations of proposition correspondence

Continued

3.3. Identification and classification of proposition correspondence
3.4. Q&A
4. Pilot assessment
4.1. The 1st round, PA assessment of 10 sentences, followed by a 5-minute break
4.2. The 2nd round, PA assessments of 4 paragraphs, followed by a 10-minute break
4.3. Q&A, discussion
5. Wrapping-up (concluding the training)

Phase 2 rater training takes place 3 weeks after the accomplishment of Phase 1 assessment. The rating training session follows the principle of "minimum training". That is, the trainer only provides necessary information to the raters. The training procedure is listed below in Table 4.6. During the training session, the trainer explains the EIC scale and assessment sheet and the weighted score of each segment, stressing that raters should only rate information fidelity, regardless of other criteria. When the raters are sure of the information, 5 anchored recordings are played for pilot assessment. The raters are reminded that these recordings demonstrate different levels of information fidelity, but exact scores will not be given. When the raters have different ideas, they could discuss about them. Similar to discussion in Phase 1, rater does not discuss rating scores of the anchored recordings.

Table 4.6 Phase 2: Rater Training Procedure

1. Warm-up (ethics clearance, rapport-building)
2. Rating introduction, followed by a 5-minute break
2.1. Rating materials
2.2. Assessment procedure

Continued

3. EIC-based assessment, followed by a 10-minute break
3.1. Assessment scale and sheet
3.2. Weighted scores of segments
3.3. Q&A
4. Pilot assessment, followed by a 5-minute break
4.1. Five anchored recordings
4.2. Q&A, discussion
5. Wrapping-up (concluding the training)

4.5 Principles of PA

4.5.1 Proposition as an Assessment Unit of Information Fidelity

The information assessment unit is essential for the assessment of information fidelity in interpreting performance. Information units include information point, information stratum and information structure. (Cai, 2003) Based on the criterion, proposition has the potential to serve as a basic information assessment unit.

Based on the concept of proposition and propsitional relations, proposition can meet the demand for an information assessment unit. First, proposition itself, as a basic unit of semantic meaning representation, embodies information units proposed by Cai (2003). Second, the propositional correspondence relations represent the logical relations among information points, which means that PA could reprensent the information stratum. Third, propositions and proposition relations, when combined together, form the text base, which reveals the macro-strucutre of text. Thus, PA provides a hierarchical frame for information fidelity assessment, inclusive of all the information units that are required in interpreting performance assessment. Furthermore, PA boasts of a set of coding schemes to detect, identify and classify propositional correspondece between the source text and interpreted text. With that said, it is fair to consider proposition as a basic information assessment unit in interpreting performance test.

In this study, the PA-based criterion takes proposition as a basic assessment unit of information fidelity. A proposition consists of two basic components: Predicate, and Argument(s). The rules of propositionalization, detection and classification of propositional correspondence are based on Yeh (2015), Bovair & Kieras (1981) and Kintsch & van Djik (1978), which are to be introduced in detail below.

4.5.2 Classifications of Propositional Correspondence

Raters use PA as a scoring criterion, that is, to find out whether propositions in TL texts are semantically in correspondence with propositions in SL texts and classify the category of correspondence. Based on identification and classification methods of Yeh (2015), Porter (2006), Kintsch & van Djik (1978), Bovair & Kieras (1981), the author adapts and abbreviates the description format of propositions for the convenience of assessment. Propositions in this study are organized and described with the following principles (adapted from Bovair & Kieras, 1981: 4-6):

① When there are various reasonable ways to represent the text, choose the simplest;

② Try to avoid embedding and simplify scoring;

③ Represent compound nouns as a single term;

④ Avoid unnecessary variants of terms.

Propositions in the study have three different types: The first type of propositions refers to standard propositions with Predicate, Argument 1, Argument 2; The rest two types are propositions with Predicate, Argument 1 or Argument 1, Argument 2. In the structure of (Predicate, Argument 1), Predicate is usually represented by an intransitive verb. In the structure of (Argument 1, Argument 2), it is perhaps a list or a modification.

1. (Predicate, Argument 1, Argument 2):

   a. The cat eats the mouse.   (EAT, CAT, MOUSE)

   b. 我在写论文。   （写，我，论文）

2. (Predicate, Argument 1):

   a. He arrives.   (ARRIVE, HE)

   b. 他胜利了。   （胜利，他）

3. （Argument 1, Argument 2, ...)

   a. Japan, U.S.   (Japan, U.S.)

   b. 太好了。   （好，太）

For the TL and SL propositions, their semantic correspondence could be identified with the following four categories:

① no semantic correspondence;

② one semantic correspondence (Predicate or Argument 1 or Argument 2);

③ two semantic correspondence (Predicate and Argument 1, or Predicate and Argument 2, or Argument 1 and Argument 2);

④ Complete semantic correspondence (Predicate, Argument 1, Argument 2). (adapted from Yeh, 2015: 16)

The correspondence classification could also be used to identify Type 2 and Type 3 propositions.

The classification of correspondence could tell principles of correspondence:

First components of propositions in TL texts should correspond to components in SL text. (Three to three, or two to two. If there are three components in SL text, while there are only two in TL text, then it belongs to "omission". If there are two components in SL text, while there are three in TL text, then it belongs to "addition".)

For example:

Match in number:

SL text: China became the world's largest smartphone market.

P1: (BECOME, CHINA, P2)

P2: (LARGEST, SM MARKET, WORLD)

TL text: 中国成为世界最大的智能手机市场。

P1:(成为,中国,P2)

P2:(最大,智能手机市场,世界)

Omission:

SL text: Mobile is also driving intense innovation in the start-up community.

P1:(DRIVE, MOBILE, P2)

P2:(INNOVATE, START-UP COMMUNITY)

TL text: 移动技术促进了创新。

P1:(促进,移动技术,创新)

Addition:

SL text: It's a privilege for me to speak about mobile technologies.

P1: (SPEAK, PRIVILEGE, MT)

TL text: 我很荣幸来这里讲讲移动技术带来的影响。

P1:(荣幸,我,P2)

P2:(讲,我,P3)

P3:(带来,移动技术,影响)

Second, When components are matching in number (three vs. three), and when only two components are semantically corresponding (Predicate and Argument 1, or Predicate and Argument 2, or Argument 1 and Argument 2), we should categorize them into "match".

For example:

SL text: China became the world's largest smartphone market.

P1: (BECOME, CHINA, P2)

P2: (LARGEST, SM MARKET, WORLD)

TL text: 中国成为最大的智能手机市场。

P1:(成为，中国，P2)

P2:(最大，智能手机市场)

Third, When components are matching in number (two vs. two), only when one component is semantically corresponding, we categorize them into "correspondence". In the following example, P2 in SL text is (cold, coffee), and P2 in TL text is (热，咖啡). Argument 1 matches, so P2 is categorized into "match".

For example:

SL text: China is now home to more innovators in mobile technology than any other country other than the U.S. and Republic of Korea.

P1: (BECOME, CHINA, P2)

P2: (3RD LARGESTS COUNTRY, CHINA, MT)

P3: (AFTER, U.S., S.K.)

TL text: 中国现在是世界上最大的创新国。

P1:(是，中国，P2)

P2:(最大，创新国，世界上)

Fourth, When all the components are semantically equivalent, the proposition belongs to match; when two or more components are not semantically equivalent, it belongs to "unmatch".

4.5.3 Propositionalization Procedure

The present investigation adopts a propositionalization procedure based on a four-step procedure proposed by Turner & Greene (1977) and Bovair & Kieras (1981). The procedure is listed below in Table 4.7, which details propositionalization on the sentential basis.

Table 4.7 Propositionalization Procedure

1. Loosely parse the sentence into clauses	
2. Pick out connectives	
3. For main clause	**a.** Represent main verb as Predicate and Arguments
	b. Represent modifiers of Predicate
	c. Represent modifiers to Arguments
	d. Represent modifiers to other propositions
4. Repeat a—d for the subordinate clauses	

The following is an example of propositionalization of a sentence in the source speech:

SL sentence: Facebook alone grew 78 percent year-over-year between 2009 and 2013, with mobile currently representing 88 percent of its user base and accounting for approximately 66 percent of its revenue.

Step 1: Loosely parse the sentence into clauses.

Facebook alone grew 78 percent year-over-year//between 2009 and 2013//, with mobile currently representing 88 percent of its user base//and accounting for approximately 66 percent of its revenue.//

Step 2: Pick out connectives.

Facebook alone grew 78 percent//year-over-year//*between* 2009 *and* 2013//, *with* mobile currently representing 88 percent of its user base//*and* accounting for approximately 66 percent of its revenue.//

Step 3: Main clause propositionalization

a. Represent main verb as Predicate and Arguments.

Facebook grew 78%: P1 (GROW, FB, 78%)

b. Represent modifiers of Predicate.

Facebook grew 78% year-over-year: P2 (yearly, P1)

c. Represent modifiers to other propositions.

between 2009 *and* 2013: P3 (BETWEEN ... AND ..., 2009, 2013)

With the analysis, propositions of the main clause of this sentence are:

P1: (GROW, FB, 78%)

P2: (YEARLY, P1)

P3: (BETWEEN ... AND ..., 2009, 2013)

Repeating the procedure, we can get all the rest clauses propositionalized:

P1: (GROW, FB, 78%)

P2: (yearly, P1)

P3: (BETWEEN ... AND ..., 2009, 2013)

P4: (REPRESENT, MOBILE, USER BASE)

P5: (USER BASE, 88%)

P6: (ACCOUNT FOR, MOBILE, REVENUE)

P7: (REVENUE, ABOUT 66%)

The rest of the source text and the interpreted texts are all propositionalized in this way.

4.5.4 Coding Scheme of Propositional Correspondence

Based on Yeh's coding scheme (2015), the researcher stipulates a coding scheme (Table 4.8) used in the present investigation, only considering categories of propositional correspondence when taking the source text as reference.

Table 4.8 Coding Scheme of PA

Match		
No.	Code	Explanation
1	M	Complete Match
2	M-PREED	Match-Meaning Presupposed
3	M-ENTED	Match-Meaning Entailed
Match-Unclear		
No.	Code	Explanation
1	M-U-PREING	Match-Unclear-Meaning Presupposing
2	M-U-ENTING	Match-Unclear-Meaning Entailing
3	M-ALTED	Match-Meaning Altered
Mismatch		
No.	Code	Explanation
1	A-PSVED	Addition-Meaning Preserved
2	A-ALTED	Addition-Meaning Altered
3	O-PSVED	Omission-Meaning Preserved
4	O-ALTED	Omission-Meaning Altered

In interpreting assessment, P1 is a proposition in the source text. Therefore, it is eternal truth. We will only consider situations in which P1 is of truth value. Therefore, in the coding scheme, the author will use P1 as the benchmark to match the degree of correspondence of P2. Synonym means that P1 and P2 are matching in semantic information, so it is categorized in the group "Match". Contradiction means that P1 and P2 will never match in information, so it is categorized in the group of "Mismatch". Now the complex part is the categorization of entailment and presupposition. Based on Yeh's scheme (2015), the author summarizes three categories—Match, Match-Unclear, and Mismatch, using source text as a benchmark of assessment.

The working procedure of the coding scheme is presented hereafter:

S1: The rapid diffusion of mobile technologies in the first decade of the new millennium has little precedent in history.

T1: 在过去的十年间,移动技术得到了前所未有的发展,这是之前所没有的。

First, the author propositionalizes these two sentences, and then we get Table 4.9 and Table 4.10:

Table 4.9 Propositionalizing S1's Sentence

P1	FIRST	DECADE	
P2	P1	NEW MILLENIUM	
P3	RAPID	DIFFUSION	
P4	MOBILE TECH	P3	
P5	LITTLE	PRECEDENT	HISOTRY
P6	HAS	P4	P5

Table 4.10 Propositionalizing T1's Sentence

P1	过去	十年	
P2	前所未有的	发展	
P3	得到	移动技术	P2
P4	没有	P3	之前

Second, propositions of the source text and the interpreted text are put in ".xls" file, for propositional correspondence identification and classification (see Table 4.11):

Table 4.11 Samples of Proposition

No.	PREDICATE	ARGUMENT 1	ARGUMENT 2	Category	No.	PREDICATE	ARGUMENT 1	ARGUMENT 2
P1	FIRST	DECADE			P1	过去	十年	
P2	P1	NEW MILLENIUM			P2			
P3	RAPID	DIFFUSION			P3	前所未有的	发展	
P4	MOBILE TECH	P3						
P5	LITTLE	PRECEDENT	HISOTRY		P3	前所未有的	发展	
P6	HAS	P4	P5		P4	得到	移动技术	P2
					P5	没有	P4	之前

Then, the propositional correspondence on the left and the right columns are analyzed, and categorized (see Table 4.12):

Table 4.12 Samples of Propositional Correspondence

No.	PREDICATE	ARGUMENT 1	ARGUMENT 2	Category	No.	PREDICATE	ARGUMENT 1	ARGUMENT 2
P1	FIRST	DECADE		M-ALTED	P1	过去	十年	
P2	P1	NEW MILLENIUM		O-ALTED	P2			
P3	RAPID	DIFFUSION		M-PREED	P3	前所未有的	发展	
P4	MOBILE TECH	P3		M				
P5	LITTLE	PRECEDENT	HISOTRY	M	P3	前所未有的	发展	
P6	HAS	P4	P5	M	P4	得到	移动技术	P2
				A-PSVED	P5	没有	P4	之前

Third, count the number of each category and calculate the rate of information fidelity, which is then the score of information fidelity of this sentence (see Table 4.13).

Table 4.13 The Score of Information Fidelity of This Sentence

No. of Proposition	Category	No. of Category	No. of Accpt.	Rate
7	Match	3	4	57%
	M-ALTED	1		
	O-ALTED	1		
	M-PREED	1		
	A-PSVED	1		

4.6 Rating Procedure

Raters are required to mark information fidelity of the sample materials twice, following two different assessment criteria: firstly based on PA and then on the EIC criterion. To mitigate potential impact of Phase 1 on Phase 2, several measures are taken:

① Two tasks are carried out with an interval of three weeks, so that Phase 2 rating will not be affected by the "carryover effect" of Phase 1 rating.

② The list of examinees is randomized for each rater and at each phase. Raters are not likely to recognize the files, even when they are assessing the same materials they worked on weeks ago. After all, the two phases are adopting different forms of assessment.

③ Raters work at home or office separately. They do not discuss the assessment issues with each other.

Raters identify the correspondence of propositions between the source text and the target text, together with their semantic relations. At the end of each text, numbers of propositions that are considered loyal to those in the source text are counted and a score is given. Meanwhile, numbers of categories are collected for further research.

Three weeks after the PA-based assessment, raters start to work with the

EIC criterion. Raters will be given the source text in English and assessment sheets of EIC. Each segment is assigned with a weighted score in accordance with information density. Raters then listen to the audios and give a score of information fidelity after each segment. At the end of each audio, they calculate all scores of the seven segments and give a total score of information fidelity.

After rating, scoring results are collected, which are input into and analyzed by software (SPSS and FACETS) for statistical analysis. Scores are measured statistically from the following perspectives:

① inter-rater reliability of PA rating;

② inter-rater reliability of EIC rating;

③ correlation analysis of PA rating and EIC rating;

④ rater severity/leniency with PA rating and EIC rating;

⑤ rater effects of PA rating and EIC rating;

⑥ rater bias of PA rating and EIC rating.

4.7 Summary

This chapter presents some basic components of the experiment designed to measure reliability and validity of PA in interpreting assessment. Some forty MTI trainees take part in the experiment and an English speech is used as the test material, which is examined by Coh-Metrix to be suitable in terms of difficulty index. To validate PA, the detailed propositionalization and classification of propositions are described in this chapter. Three raters are recruited to assess information fidelity of examinees' performance twice, one with the PA-based criterion and the other with the EIC criterion. In addition to quantitative work, learners' questionnaires are also studied to find clues for self-perception of the existing problems and hopes for teachers and future study. All these provide concrete and instrumental data for the discussion of pedagogical implications in Chapter 6.

Chapter 5

Validation of the PA-Based Assessment of Information Fidelity in Consecutive Interpreting

Previously, propositional analysis, an instrument for the assessment of information fidelity, has been proposed and explored theoretically, in terms of applicability in interpreting tests. This chapter is mainly about the validation of this newly-proposed assessment criterion. At the beginning, a prevailing tool-kit in language assessment—Multi-Faceted Rasch Measurement (MFRM)—is introduced, together with a software (FACETS) that helps with its data analysis. Then, MFRM and FACETS are used to validate the PA-based criterion with evidence from three perspectives: construct validity, criterion validity and rater reliability. The last part of the chapter consists of data analysis extracted from the PA-based assessment, in comparison with the results based on the EIC criterion, which offers empirical evidence for pedagogical discussion in the following chapter.

5.1 MFRM: Preparation for Validation

It is widely acknowledged that in language testing and assessment, it involves "a large and diverse set of procedures to measure language ability or some aspect of that ability" (Eckes, 2015:15). The situation is more complex and exhausting in interpreting assessment, in which co-functioning factors that need careful consideration are a lot more than those in written or reading tests, such as settings, participants, delivery, tone and voice, even target audience. Further, it is difficult to tell whether the test is valid in measuring examinee ability. On the other hand, "the error-prone nature of most measurement facets" (Eckes, 2015: 17), or volatility in human rating, which greatly undermines rating reliability, has been a constant concern of psychometrics. In this regard, an adequate approach to analyze the complex language assessment and mitigate rater bias or preference is anxiously desired. In this respect, MFRM arises to answer the call.

Rasch Model was proposed by George Rasch, a Danish statistician, in 1960. Originally, it was intended to analyze responses to multiple-choice items; that is, examinee's response to it could either be correct or wrong. Rasch Model measures probability that examinees make the correct choice, determined by item difficulty and examinee ability. The relations among ability, item difficulty and probability of success in this typical dichotomous Rasch Model could be seen with item characteristic curves in Figure 5.1.

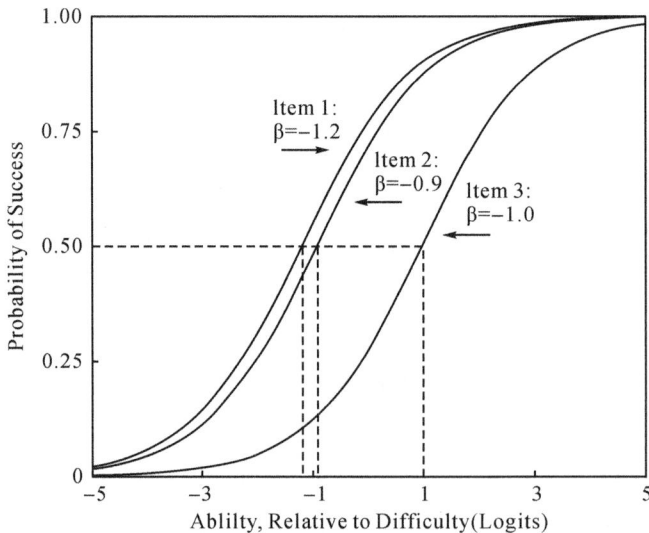

Figure 5.1 Item Characteristic Curves for Item Difficulty and Ability (After Eckes, 2015: 23)

The horizontal axis represents examinee ability (θ values), relative to item difficulty (β values). The vertical axis represents the probability of success, ranging from 0 to 1. The rationale behind this S-shaped curve is that for an item, the probability of success increases as examinee ability increases. The values along the horizontal axis is exp(θ−β). The S-shaped curve is a result of equation of exponential index:

$$P_{ni} = \frac{\exp\left(\theta_n - \beta_i\right)}{1 + \exp\left(\theta_n - \beta_i\right)}$$

P_{ni}= probability of examinee n anwers item i correctly

θ_n = ability of examinee n

β_i = difficulty of item i

The equation represents Rasch Model. A major advantage of Rasch Model lies in its success of measuring ability and item difficulty on a common measurable scale. The scale uses *logit* as its basic unit. The horizontal axis in Figure 5.1 covers an expansion of 10 logits (−5 to 5), or 5 interval categories. For example, for Item 3, β_3=1. When ability matches item difficulty (θ_3=1), then $\left(\theta_3 - \beta_3\right) = 0$. And $\exp(0) = 1$. So, the corresponding probability of success on the vertical axis is 0.5, which means examinees' probability, measured against their ability, to choose the correct answer of Item 3 is 50%. When ability is lower than difficulty, we should move along the horizontal axis to the left, which means the probability of success is lower than 0.5. When ability is higher than difficulty, we should move along the horizontal axis to the right, and the probability of right answer is higher than 0.5.

Another distinctive advantage of Rasch Model analysis lies in its measurement invariance of item and trait parameters; that is, in a Rasch Model, examinee measures are invariant regardless of various sets of items, and item measures are invariant regardless of various groups of examinees. Then, examinee measures are "item-free or test-free", and item measures are "examinee-free, or sample-free" (Wright, 1999; Eckes, 2015). This trait of Rasch Model makes up for the drawbacks of previous assessment tools, for which examinee ability and test difficulty are inter-related and inter-dependent. No doubt that Rasch Model is a huge advance for language assessment.

As mentioned previously, early Rasch Model was developed for analyzing multiple-choice-item part of the test. The aforementioned Rasch Model considers ability and item difficulty only. This dichotomous model is uni-dimensional, which measures only one latent ability. When it comes to speaking or interpreting, more latent abilities (fluency, delivery, expression, etc.) come to the fore. Further, more factors in assessment such as tasks, domains, raters, criteria and scales, all call for our concern. Then, the dichotomous Rasch Model extends to modeling polytomous items, considering many facets of language assessment at the same time. A frequently applied Rasch Model is known as Multi-Faceted Rasch Measurement (MFRM), developed by Linacre in 1994. Linacre extends the Model from two facets (item difficulty and examinee ability) to many facets (including but not exhaustive of raters, tasks, domains, scales and criteria).

In addition to the characteristics of Rasch Model, MFRM boasts of some distinctive merits. First and foremost, MFRM could sort out the factors that affect test performance, turn them into parameters and integrate them into the model. Figure 5.2 illustrates MFRM of translation performance tests.

This framework illustrates some principal components that MFRM focuses on: ability, rater effect (halo effect, severity, neutralization, etc.), task difficulty, rating difficulty and rating scale/criterion. The rationale of MFRM goes in this way: Based on raw score analysis, the Rasch Model would create some expected estimates for each component, if the observed scores fall within the range of the expected estimates, they are considered to fit the Model estimates. For instance, if scores from a rater fit the Rasch Model estimates, and unexpected responses are few, we can say that the rater has high intra-rater reliability. If scores from a group of raters fit the estimates range and unexpected responses are few, they achieve high inter-rater reliability. Similar conclusions could be made in terms of examinee ability, task difficulty and criterion. To some degree, this achievement offers empirical evidence to confirm criterion validity of the test.

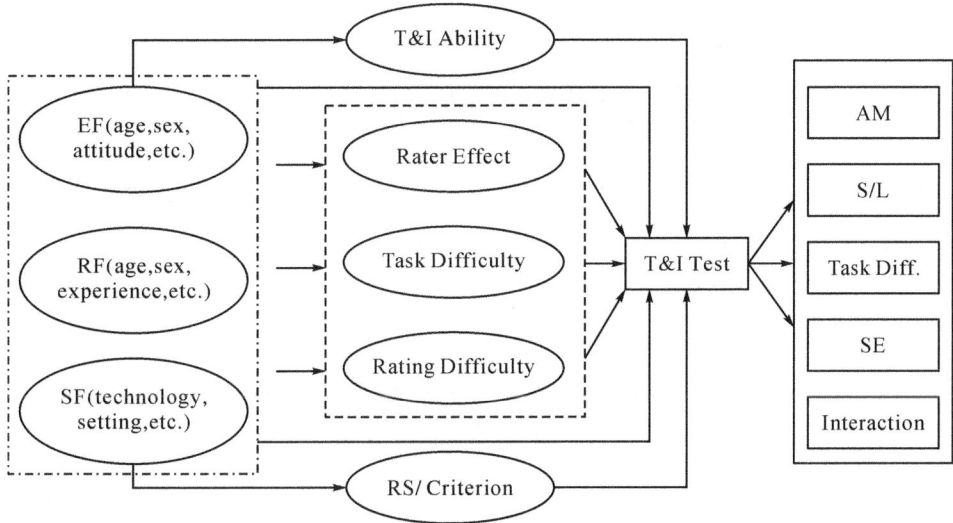

Figure 5.2 Framework of MFRM of T&I Test
(After Eckes, 2015: 49; Zhang, 2017: 78)

Note: EF = Examinee Features; RF = Rater Features; ST = Setting Features;
T&I = Translation and Interpreting; RS = Rating Scale;
AM= Ability Measure; S/L = Severity/Leniency; Task Diff. = Task Difficulty; SE = Scale Effect

Factors on the left column of the Figure, examinee features, rater features and settings features are some factors that affect test score indirectly. Examinee features include age, sex, ethnic group, attitude, etc. Rater features include age, sex, ethnic group, education and work experiences, motivations, etc. Settings include technological issues and environment when the test takes place.

Factors on the rightmost column are measurements of factors after MFRM, including ability measure, rater severity/leniency, task difficulty, scale effect and interaction.

Eckes' framework paves the way for validation procedure in T&I assessment targeting rater effects, examinee ability and test-related indicators, which could also extend to other kinds of tests. Based on the framework, Zhang (2017) proposes a MFRM framework for her newly-proposed analytic rating scale of Chinese-English translation competence test, which is shown in Figure 5.3

Zhang claims that validation procedure of a scale or criterion could be accomplished by collecting evidence from three aspects: construct validity, criterion validity and rater reliability. While construct validity could be validated in theoretical domain, criterion validity and rater reliability could best be empirically validated. This part of validation needs evidence from several aspects:

① correlation analysis of the proposed and existing scales/criteria;

② inter-rater reliability of the scales/criteria;

③ score discrepancy of the scales/criteria;

④ comparison of data discrepancies from the dimension of examinees, raters, scales/criteria, interaction of examinees and raters, interaction between raters and scales/criteria.

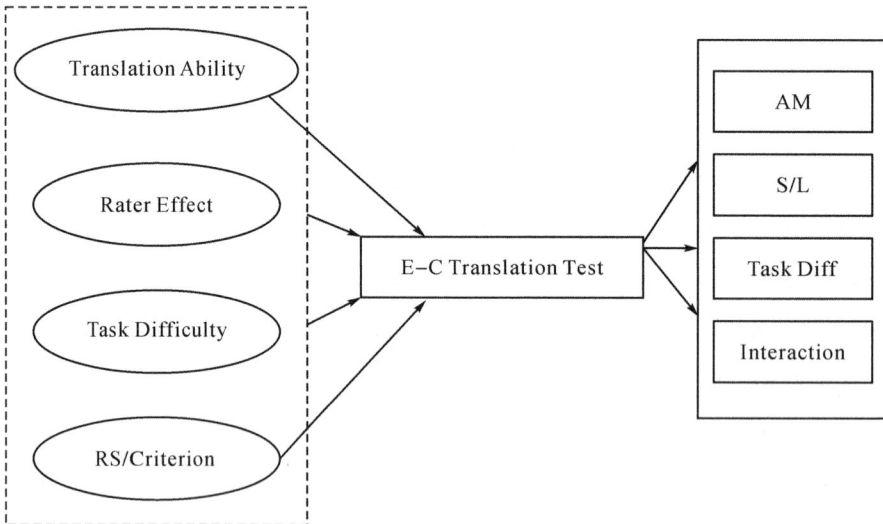

Figure 5.3 A MFRM-Based Framework of Analytic Rating Scale for C-E Translation Competence Test (After Zhang, 2017: 79)

The present study follows Zhang's trail in deploying MFRM into the PA-based assessment of information fidelity. Adapted from Zhang's framework, a MFRM framework of the PA-based assessment of information fidelity is constructed, which is illustrated in Figure 5.4.

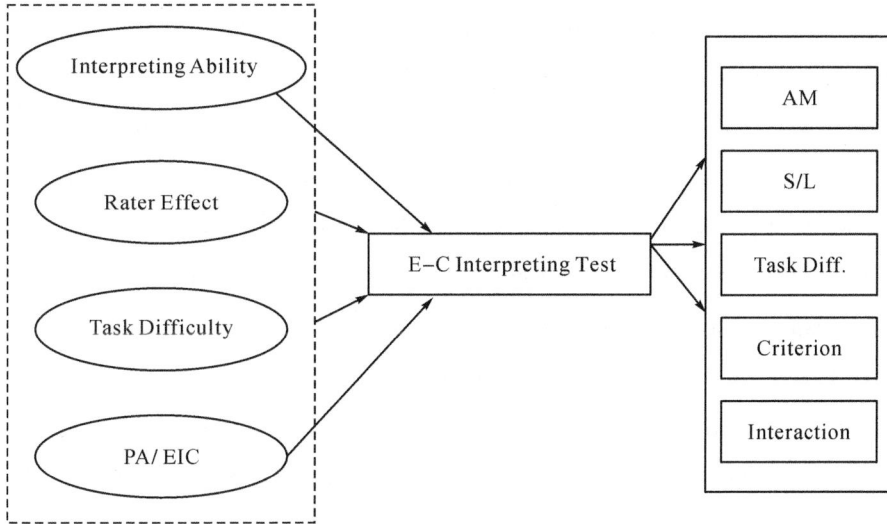

Figure 5.4 A MFRM-Based Framework of the Assessment of Information Fidelity in Interpreting Test

To validate the proposed PA-based criterion in the assessment of information fidelity, this study will extract data from scores of information fidelity with two criteria (the PA-based criterion and the EIC criterion). The validation process is realized by collecting evidence of three perspectives: construct validity, criterion validity and rating validity. Empirical evidence concerning the above dimensions will be gathered by means of the statistical analysis procedure① listed below:

① correlation analysis of the PA-based scores and the EIC scores;

② inter-rater and intra-rater reliability of the PA-based scores and the EIC scores;

③ score discrepancy of the PA-based scores and the EIC scores;

④ comparison of data discrepancy from the dimensions of examinee, rater, criterion, and interaction of rater-criterion pairs.

Of the three-dimension evidence necessary in this PA-based criterion validation, construct validity, namely, theoretical discussion of propositional analysis in the assessment of information fidelity, has been accomplished in Chapter 4. Therefore, this chapter mainly focuses on collecting empirical evidence of the rest two aspects: criterion validity and rater reliability.

Criterion validity refers to the degree to which a measure is related to an outcome. (Weir, 2005) In this study, criterion validity refers to the degree to which the PA-based criterion is related to the outcome of information fidelity assessment.

---

① In psychometrics, a proposed scale/criterion could be validated by collecting evidence from three perspectives: construct validity, criterion validity and rating validity (or rater reliability).(Zhang, 2017) Construct validity refers to the degree to which a test measures what it claims, or purports, to be measuring. (Cronbach & Meehl, 1955) Criterion validity refers to the degree to which a measure is related to an outcome. The criterion measure can be validated concurrently, that is, whether the test results correlate when examinees' performance is assessed with different scales/ criteria. In this sense, criterion validity could be validated through comparing rating results from different criteria. In the present study, criterion validity is measured by means of correlation analysis of the scores from the PA-based criterion and the EIC criterion. Rating validity, or rater reliability, refers to the degree to which rating behavior is unbiased, or related to test performance. "One important type of statistical evidence that indicates rater unbiasedness and reliability of rating behavior is rater reliability estimates ..., (which) fall into three broad categories: (a) consensus estimates; (b) consistency estimates and measurement estimates". (Han, 2015: 50–53) Consensus estimates and consistency estimates could be measured through intra- and inter-rater consistency indices with SPSS analysis. Measurement estimates could be measured through rater bias index with Rasch analysis. (Knoch & Chapelle, 2017)

Rating validity, or rater reliability, refers to the degree to which rating behavior is unbiased, or related to test performance. (Zhang, 2017) In the present study, rating validity refers to the degree to which rating behavior is unbiased, or related to test performance, on the PA-based criterion, or the EIC criterion.

After the design of MFRM framework, it is time to choose appropriate Rasch Models for the investigation. Eckes (2009) summarizes some major multi-faceted Rasch Models for language assessment, determined by the parameters or facets that researchers intend to explore. These facets include examinee ability, criterion difficulty, rater severity/leniency, step difficulty, task difficulty, interaction, etc. It should be noted that the parameters listed are not exhaustive. Researchers and examiners could put in or remove some parameters, depending on study purposes.

For the evidence required in the present study, Step 1 and Step 2 could be accomplished with the help of SPSS.

Step 3 and Step 4 deploy MFRM analysis. The author chooses two Rasch Models for this purpose. For Step 3, the author adopts a 2-parameter Rasch Model:

$$\ln\left(\frac{P_{njk}}{P_{nj(k-1)}}\right) = \theta_n - \alpha_j - \tau_k$$

P_{njk} = probability of examinee n receiving a rank of k from rater j;

$P_{nj(k-1)}$ = probability of examinee n receiving a rank of $k-1$ from rater j;

θ_n = ability of examinee n;

α_j = severity of rater j;

τ_k = difficulty of receiving a rating of k relative to $k-1$.

The second Rasch Model is for Step 4, which is a 3-parameter model:

$$\ln\left(\frac{P_{nijk}}{P_{nij(k-1)}}\right) = \theta_n - \beta_i - \alpha_j - \tau_k$$

P_{nijk} = probability of examinee n receiving a rank of k from rater j on criterion i;

$P_{nij(k-1)}$ = probability of examinee n receiving a rank of $k-1$ from rater j on criterion i;

θ_n = ability of examinee n;

β_i = difficulty of criterion i;

α_j = severity of rater j;

τ_k = difficulty of receiving a rating of k relative to $k-1$.

These validation steps require vast amount of computation capacity. The study employs software like SPSS and FACETS to conduct data analysis and realize data visualization of the outcomes. SPSS and FACETS are to be briefly discussed in the next section.

5.2 SPSS and FACETS Analysis

This study will apply statistical software to data analysis: SPSS and FACETS.

SPSS (Statistical Product and Service Solutions) is to conduct data analysis in terms of mean score, standard deviance, Kendall consistency efficient of inter-rater reliability, LSD and ANOVO Post-hoc tests.

FACETS is a major software for MFRM, developed by Linacre in the 1990s. Owing to the complexity and requirements for huge capability of computation of some scientific studies, MFRM is mostly computer-aided. The software FACETS is developed for this purpose. FACETS makes estimation of parameters on the basis of Unconditional Maximum Likelihood, projected the data in the form of *logits*, a unit of measurement in MFRM. Then estimation outcomes could evaluate the fit statistics of every facet. Fit statistics tells us characteristics of raw data, such as rater consistency, unexpected responses, ability, etc. Before data processing and analysis, it is necessary to explain some key terms in FACETS.

5.2.1 Measure

Measure stands for the level of examinee ability in FACETS. *Logit* is the basic unit of measure. In Table 5.1, measure contains 8 *logits* (−3 to 4), which tells the discrepancy of ability among students. Examinee with the highest ability is 3.24 *logits*, examinee with the lowest ability is −2.82 *logits*, then the best and worst students expand 6.06 *logits* in ability.

Table 5.1 FACETS Data 1

```
-----------------------------------------------------------------
|Measr|+raters|-criteria            |-examinees|-items|Scale|
-----------------------------------------------------------------
+   4 +       +                      +          +      + (5) +
|     |       |                      |          |      |     |
|     |       |                      |          |      |     |
|     |       |                      |   *      |      |     |
|     |       |                      |          |      |     |
+   3 +       +                      +          +      +     +
|     |       |                      |          |      |     |
|     |       |                      |          |      |     |
|     |       |                      |   *      |      | --- |
|     |       |                      |          |      |     |
+   2 +       +                      +          +      +     +
|     |       |                      |   *      |      |     |
|     |       |                      |          |      |  4  |
|     |       |                      |   *      |      |     |
|     |       |                      |   *      |      |     |
|     |       |                      |   *      |      |     |
+   1 +       +                      +   *      +      + --- +
|     |       |                      |   *      |      |     |
|     |       |                      |  ****  3 |      |     |
|     |       |                      |  ***     |      |  3  |
|     |       |                      |  ***   4 5      |     |
|     |       |                      |  ****    |      |     |
|     | XR    | PA-based analysis    |  **      |      | --- |
*   0 * YHB   *                      *          *      *     *
|     | HJ    | XMUEIC               |  ***   2 |      |     |
|     |       |                      |  **    6 |      |  2  |
|     |       |                      |  **    7 |      |     |
|     |       |                      |  ***     |      |     |
|     |       |                      |  *     1 |      |     |
|     |       |                      |  *       |      | --- |
+  -1 +       +                      + **       +      +     +
|     |       |                      |          |      |     |
|     |       |                      |   *      |      |  1  |
|     |       |                      |  **      |      |     |
+  -2 +       +                      +          +      +     +
|     |       |                      |          |      |     |
|     |       |                      |   *      |      | --- |
|     |       |                      |          |      |     |
|     |       |                      |   *      |      |     |
|     |       |                      |   *      |      |     |
+  -3 +       +                      +          +      + (0) +
-----------------------------------------------------------------
|Measr|+raters|-criteria            | * = 1    |-items|Scale|
-----------------------------------------------------------------
```

5.2.2 Separation Ratio, Separation Index and Reliability of Separation Index

Separation ratio indicates that the ratio between actual examinee difference in ability and measure deviation. The higher the ratio is, the more likely that ability of examinees is significantly different. In Table 5.2, separation ratio is 6.77; that is, the actual ability gap among examinees is 6.7 times more than estimation. It means that examinees are significantly different in interpreting ability of message transfer.

Separation index means the number of distinct strata based on examinees' ability. It could be calculated in this way: (4G+1)/3 (G: separation ratio). In Table 5.1, the separation index of examinees is (4×6.77+1)/3 = 9, meaning that on an ability basis, students could be divided into 9 strata.

Reliability of separation index is similar to Cronbach alpha coefficient in Classical Test Theory (CTT). (Zhang, 2017) It represents the possibility of interpersonal discrepancy, ranging between 0 and 1. The closer it is to 1, the more likely that there exists significant discrepancy among students. In Table 5.2, reliability of separation index is 0.98, showing that students are most likely to be significantly different in interpreting ability.

Table 5.2 FACETS Data 2

Obsvd Score	Obsvd Count	Obsvd Average	Fair-M Average	Measure	Model SE	Infit		Outfit		Estim. Discrm	Nu Examinees
						MnSq	Zstd	MnSq	Zstd		
100.1	42.0	2.4	2.37	0	0.17	1.02	−0.3	1.04	−0.3		Mean (Count:44)
43.6	0	1.0	1.07	1.20	0.03	0.52	2.3	0.56	2.3		SD (Populn.)
44.1	0	1.1	1.08	1.21	0.03	0.53	2.3	0.56	2.3		SD (Sample)
Model, Populn: RMSE 0.18 Adj (True) SD 1.19 Separation 6.77 Reliability 0.98											

Continued

Obsvd Score	Obsvd Count	Obsvd Average	Fair-M Average	Measure	Model SE	Infit		Outfit		Estim. Discrm	Nu Examinees
						MnSq	Zstd	MnSq	Zstd		
Model, Sample: RMSE 0.18 Adj (True) SD 1.20 Separation 6.85 Reliability 0.98											
Model, Fixed (all same) Chi-Square: 1467.0 df: 43 Significance (probability) 0											
Model, Random (normal) Chi-Square: 41.5 df: 42 Significance (probability) 0.49											

The three terms introduced are used in every facet, it could not only separate examinees in terms of ability, but also raters in terms of severity and criterion difficulty.

5.2.3 Chi-Square Statistics and Significance

Chi-square statistics, like separation ratio index, implies individual difference in every facet. Significance is more like separation ratio index, ranging from 0 to 1. If significance value of an experiment is less than 0.05, we can conclude that statistical difference exists among subjects.

5.2.4 Fit Statistics

Fit statistics values the extent to which the observed score fits the estimated value in the matrix. FACETS provides two types of fit statistics: infit and outfit. Of which, the infit statistics are "the ones usually considered the most informative, as they focus on the degree of fit in the most typical observations in the matrix" (McNamara, 1996:172). The outfit statistics are subject to be affected by extreme scores.

Both infit and outfit statistics contain 2 terms: mean square (MnSq) and Zstd. MnSq ranges from 0 to ∞. When MnSq is 1, it means the observed score matches the matrix perfectly. When MnSq is below 1, it means the two overfit. When MnSq is more than 1, it means the two misfit. McNamara (2002) suggests that MnSq value fluctuating between 0.5—1.5 be considered acceptable. But when it comes to high-stakes assessment, the range should be further narrowed.

Zstd is like *t*-test in SPSS, which indicates whether the observed scores significantly misfit, overfit or unfit to the matrix. It ranges from −2 to 2. If Zstd value is less than −2, it means a significant misfit situation occurs; if the value is higher than 2, it means a significant overfit.

MnSq in various facets means differently. In the examinee facet, MnSq indicates examinees' consistency in response. The unexpected responses could result from either examinees' performance or rater assessment.

MnSq in the rater facet shows rating consistency, similar to intra-rater reliability in Classical Test Theory. (Myford & Wolfe, 2000) If MnSq value falls within the range of 0.5 and 1.5, it implies that raters are consistent during rating. If MnSq value falls out of the range, it implies that raters fail to follow the criterion strictly. In this case, raters may manifest several effects:

① Randomness effect—raters may be frequently severe and lenient;

② Central tendency effect—raters may score within a limited category;

③ Halo effect—raters may be affected by previous scores or criteria.

MnSq is a key indicator in the facet of scale/criterion. If MnSq value is between 0.5 and 1.5, it reflects that the scale/criterion is well-described or reasonably constructed. If the value is not within the range, it indicates that either the scale fails to provide accurate descriptors, or the criterion is redundant. In this case, bias analysis is needed in raters and scale/criterion facets.

In Table 5.2, the infit MnSq value is 1.02 with the Zstd value −0.3. These two values both fall into the "safe" range, revealing that examinees' performance is consistent in this test. If this table is about the rater facet, it indicates a high inter-rater reliability. If the table is about the scale/criterion facet, it implies that the criterion is well-designed, or descriptors are good enough for raters to reach consensus.

These terms are necessary for adequate understanding of MFRM analysis, which appear frequently hereinafter. For the present study, MFRM is necessary to evaluate inter-rater and intra-rater consistency and rater effects under the PA-based criterion and the EIC criterion. With the terms introduced, the next section is the relevant data analysis and discussion.

5.3 Validation of the PA-Based Assessment of Information Fidelity in Consecutive Interpreting

This section mainly centers around the evidence-based validation procedure of the PA-based information fidelity assessment. Evidence is collected from three aspects: construct validity, criterion validity and rating validity.

5.3.1 Construct Validity

Construct validity is the degree to which a criterion measures what it claims, or purports to be measuring. In this case, construct validity is about how the newly-proposed PA-based criterion could measure examinees' information fidelity in their interpreting performance.

As a matter of fact, the PA-based criterion has already been validated through theoretical discussion in Chapter 4. The theoretical framework therein lays a foundation for the present empirical investigation. The PA-based criterion offers a detailed and feasible set of value judgment of the information fidelity between the source text and the target texts, from the perspective of semantic meaning.

5.3.2 Criterion Validity and Rating Validity

Evidence of criterion validity and rating validity could be supported by the following statistical data:

① Correlation analysis between the PA-based criterion and the existing EIC criterion about information fidelity;

② Inter-rater reliability of the two criteria;

③ Inter-rater discrepancy of the two criteria;

④ Interface of facets: examinee; rater; criterion; rater and criterion.

Statistical Data could be analyzed with the use of SPSS. FACETS is useful for us to extract and analyze Data.

5.3.2.1 SPSS Outputs and Analysis

The section is to conduct SPSS analysis of correlation analysis, inter-rater reliability and inter-rater variances of rating scores from the PA criterion and the EIC criterion.

5.3.2.1.1 Correlation Analysis of Rating Scores

Before data analysis, rating scores from the three raters based on the PA criterion and the EIC criterion are typed into SPSS. There are 44 subjects and 3 raters. Every rater assigns fidelity score to each subject's performance twice, one with the PA criterion and the other one with the EIC criterion. Therefore, there are altogether 264 scores, 132 scores for each criterion. Normal distribution analysis (Table 5.3) shows that for the PA-based group, Kolmogorov-Smirnov (K-S) significance is 0.11; the EIC group's K-S significance is 0.15. Both groups' K-S is above 0.05. It indicates that both groups' scores are in shape of normal distribution. Therefore, correlation analysis could carry on through Pearson Coefficient.

Table 5.3 Normal Distribution of PA and EIC Ratings

	Kolmogorov-Smirnov (K)[a]			Shapiro-Wilk		
	Stat.	df	Sig.	Stat.	df	Sig.
PA	0.094	132	0.11	0.955	132	0.313
EIC	0.084	132	0.15	0.935	132	0.423

Table 5.4 presents the outcomes of correlation analysis. The outcomes reveal that two groups of scores under PA and EIC are significantly correlated (Sig. 0.921, $p=0$), which to some extent, proves that PA-based assessment is

criterion-valid, as is EIC.

Table 5.4 Correlation of PA and EIC Ratings

	PA	EIC
PA Pearson Correlation Sig.(2-tailed)	1	0.921[**] 0.000
EIC Pearson Correlation Sig.(2-tailed)	0.921[**] 0	1

Note:"[**]": Correlation is significant at the 0.01 level (2-tailed)

5.3.2.1.2 Inter-Rater Reliability

Typically, when there are two raters involved, we could measure inter-rater reliability with Spearman Correlation Coefficient or Kappa Coefficient. When 3 or more raters are hired, we could use Kendall's coefficient of concordance (Kendall's W) for measurement (Zhang, 2017) or ANOVA analysis. This study hires 3 raters for assessment. Therefore, the author will measure inter-rater reliability with Kendall's W and Chi-square. Kendall's coefficient is usually used for measuring inter-rater consistency, ranging between 0 and 1. The higher the coefficient is, the more likely the raters are consistent with each other. Table 5.5 demonstrates Kendall's W of three raters with two criteria.

Table 5.5 Inter-Rater Reliability of PA and EIC Ratings

	PA	EIC
Kendall's W (K)[a]	0.971	0.917
Chi-Square	125.297	118.244
df	43	43
Asymp. Sig.	0	0

Statistics show that both criteria are high in inter-rater reliability, $p=0.000$, indicating that raters have reached consensus in rating performance using these two criteria. In other words, both the PA-based criterion and the EIC criterion are feasible in rating. Specifically, PA's rater-reliability is 0.971, a bit higher than EIC's 0.917. This seems to imply that PA is more likely to achieve agreement or consensus among the raters, or the raters are more probable to achieve consistency while using the PA-based criterion. The outcome is consistent with Yeh's (2015). In his study, the inter-rater reliability of PA-based assessment reaches 0.957, $p < 0.01$.

To further analyze inter-rater reliability of the two criteria, scores of each of the 7 segments are input into SPSS and computed for Kendall's W coefficient. The outputs are shown in Table 5.6.

Table 5.6 Inter-Rater Reliability of the Two Criteria in Segments

The PA-Based Criterion							
	1	2	3	4	5	6	7
Kendall's W(K)[a]	0.959	0.958	0.886	0.920	0.900	0.914	0.914
Chi-Square	123.705	126.391	114.236	118.674	116.069	117.898	118.310
df	43	43	43	43	43	43	43
Asymp. Sig.	0	0	0	0	0	0	0
The EIC Criterion							
	1	2	3	4	5	6	7
Kendall's W(K)[a]	0.915	0.851	0.800	0.842	0.854	0.857	0.819
Chi-Square	118.019	109.809	103.215	108.646	110.149	110.540	105.591
df	43	43	43	43	43	43	43
Asymp. Sig.	0	0	0	0	0	0	0

The table shows that there is no significant difference in inter-rater reliability in every segment, for either the PA-based criterion or the EIC criterion. It indicates that the raters could understand rules of the criteria and use them in rating performance in a satisfying way. However, in every segment, raters perform more consistently with the PA-based criterion than with the EIC criterion. Reliability discrepancy appears the biggest in Segment 2 (0.958 vs. 0.851) and Segment 7 (0.914 vs. 0.819), which indicates that raters with the EIC criterion are less consistent with the two segments that result in lower inter-rater reliability. In sum, the PA-based criterion appears to be more easily understood and executed by raters than the EIC criterion, although there is no significant discrepancy between the two criteria.

5.3.2.1.3 Inter-Rater Variances

The previous segment concludes that the PA-based criterion is more likely to achieve higher inter-rater reliability than the EIC criterion, which is based on rater consistency. It cannot measure inter-rater variances, though. In this segment, the author will employ ANOVA Post-hoc test to measure inter-rater variance, based on the scores of the two criteria.

Table 5.7 illustrates ANOVA analysis of the two criteria. Raters have reached similar variances when using both criteria (PA: F=0.012, p=0.998>0.05; EIC: F=1.308, p=0.274>0.05). Rater variances with PA are more homogenous (less significantly variant) than those with EIC, indicating that raters with PA achieve more consensus than with EIC.

The result is reinforced by LSD tests and ANOVA Post-hoc tests of the two criteria, presented in Table 5.7, Table 5.8 and Table 5.9.

Table 5.7 ANOVA Analysis of the Two Criteria

The PA-Based Criterion					
	Sum of Squares	D.F.	Mean Square	F	Sig.
Between Groups	1.087	2	0.543	0.012	0.988
Within Groups	5,914.496	129	45.849		
Total	5,915.583	131			

Continued

The EIC Criterion					
	Sum of Squares	df	Mean Square	F	Sig.
Between Groups	141.140	2	70.570	1.308	0.274
Within Groups	6,958.330	129	53.941		
Total	7,099.470	131			

Table 5.8 LSD Test of the Two Criteria

The PA-Based Criterion			
Levene Statistic	df1	df2	Sig.
0.087	2	129	0.917
The EIC Criterion			
Levene Statistic	df1	df2	Sig.
1.031	2	129	0.360

Table 5.9 ANOVA Post-Hoc Tests of the Two Criteria

The PA-Based Criterion					95% CI	
(I) Group	(J) Group	MD(I—J)	SE	Sig.	Lower Limit	Upper Limit
1.00	2.00	−0.2159	1.4436	0.881	−3.0721	2.6403
	3.00	−0.1536	1.4436	0.915	−3.0099	2.7026
2.00	1.00	0.2159	1.4436	0.881	−2.6403	3.0721
	3.00	0.0622	1.4436	0.966	−2.7940	2.9185
3.00	1.00	0.1536	1.4436	0.915	−2.7026	3.0099
	2.00	−0.0622	1.4436	0.966	−2.9185	2.7940

Continued

The EIC Criterion						
(I) Group	(J) Group	MD(I—J)	SE	Sig.	95%CI	
					Lower Limit	Upper Limit
1.00	2.00	2.5000	1.5658	0.113	−0.5980	5.5980
	3.00	1.6022	1.5658	0.308	−1.4958	4.7003
2.00	1.00	−2.5000	1.5658	0.113	−5.5980	0.5980
	3.00	−0.8977	1.5658	0.567	−3.9958	2.2003
3.00	1.00	−1.6022	1.5658	0.308	−4.7003	1.4958
	2.00	0.8977	1.5658	0.567	−2.2003	3.9958

LSD and post hoc test results reveal that scores of the three raters do not exist significant difference, either with the PA-based criterion ($p=0.917>0.05$), or with the EIC criterion($p=0.360>0.05$). A noteworthy finding is that the mean difference among the raters with PA (I—J: −0.2 to 0.2) fluctuates within a smaller range than that when they are with the EIC criterion (I—J: −2.5 to 2.5), showing that the raters are more consistent with each other with PA.

5.3.2.1.4 Summary of SPSS Analysis

In this section, SPSS is deployed to analyze rater performance from the perspectives of correlation analysis, inter-rater reliability and inter-rater variances. The following are some major findings of statistics analysis:

① The PA-based criterion has proved to be valid, which significantly correlates to the EIC criterion.

② The PA-based criterion could result in better inter-rater reliability than the EIC criterion, both in total scores and in segmental scores. Raters could achieve high inter-rater reliability with these two criteria, although it appears that raters with PA are more likely to achieve consistency at work.

③ LSD and post hoc test outcomes reiterate the above findings. Neither PA scores nor EIC scores exist statistical inter-rater or intra-rater significance. But PA scores fluctuate within much narrower range than EIC scores, indicating that those raters with PA perform with better consistency and stability than that when they are with the EIC criterion.

In sum, statistics reveal that both the PA-based criterion and the EIC criterion are valid for the assessment of information fidelity in consecutive interpreting, whereas the PA-based criterion is more probable to achieve higher consistency and inter-rater reliability.

5.3.2.2 FACETS Outputs and Analysis

This section is to illustrate FACETS outputs of PA-based and EIC-based scores.

5.3.2.2.1 Global FACETS Reports

Table 5.10 and Table 5.11 illustrate global FACETS reports of the PA-based criterion and the EIC criterion respectively. The first column on the left is measurement, a calibrated single linear scale to measure all the facets in *logits*: raters, examinees and segments. The logit scale "makes it possible to measure rater severity on the same scale as examinee ability, criterion difficulty and task difficulty" (Eckes, 2015: 53). The second column represents examinee ability; the higher the measure is, the better ability they perform. Examinee ability in both groups seems to be in normal distribution, minor bottom-skewed. The third column represents the rater facets; the closer raters get to the top end, the more severe they are; the closer they get to the bottom end, the more lenient they are. In Table 5.10, three raters tend to be consistent in leniency/severity. In Table 5.11, Rater A is the most severe among the three, and Rater B tends to be the most lenient, although the difference is not significant. The fourth column is segment difficulty. Both figures demonstrate that S3 is the most difficult, followed by S4 and S5, while S7 and S1 appear to be the least difficult. There is minor difference in the location of S2, S6 and S7, which is perhaps because of scale difference of the two criteria. The rightmost column reports the coverage of the scale. Scales of both criteria are similar on Level 2,3,4 and 5. In the PA-based criterion, Level 1 spans from −2.90 *logits* to −0.9 *logits*, implying that examinees whose ability falls within this range are likely to get 1 point on the scale.

Table 5.10   FACETS Report Summary of the PA-Based Criterion

```
---------------------------------------------------------------------------
|Measr|+examinees        |-raters            |-segments|Scale|
---------------------------------------------------------------------------
+   4 +                   +                   +         +  (5) +
      |                   |                   |         |      |
      |                   |                   |         |      |
      |  11               |                   |         |      |
+   3 +                   +                   +         +      +
      |                   |                   |         |      |
      |  43               |                   |         |      |
      |                   |                   |         |  --- |
+   2 +  42               +                   +         +      +
      |  44               |                   |         |      |
      |                   |                   |         |  4   |
      |  12               |                   |         |      |
      |  15   39          |                   |         |  --- |
+   1 +  37               +                   +         +      +
      |  28   32   36     |                   |         |  3   |
      |  17   29   31     |                   |  S3     |      |
      |  14   19   40     |                   |  S4  S5 |      |
      |  8                |                   |         |  --- |
      |  16   30   41   5 | Rater A  Rater B  Rater C   |      |
*   0 *  27   35          *                   *         *  2   *
      |  22   26   38     |                   |  S2     |      |
      |                   |                   |  S6     |      |
      |  18   24   33     |                   |         |      |
      |  6                |                   |  S1  S7 |      |
      |  21   9           |                   |         |  --- |
+  -1 +  1    10   4      +                   +         +      +
      |  2    34          |                   |         |      |
      |  13   23   25     |                   |         |      |
      |                   |                   |         |  1   |
+  -2 +                   +                   +         +      +
      |                   |                   |         |      |
      |  3                |                   |         |      |
      |  7                |                   |         |      |
      |                   |                   |         |  --- |
+  -3 +  20               +                   +         +      +
      |                   |                   |         |      |
      |                   |                   |         |      |
      |                   |                   |         |      |
+  -4 +                   +                   +         +  (0) +
---------------------------------------------------------------------------
|Measr|+examinees        |-raters            |-segments|Scale|
---------------------------------------------------------------------------
```

Table 5.11 FACETS Report Summary of the EIC Criterion

```
|Measr |+examinees                        |-raters  |-segments |Scale|

 +   6 +                                   +         +          + (5) +
     |                                     |         |          |     |
     |                                     |         |          |     |
 +   5 + 43                                +         +          +     +
     |                                     |         |          |     |
     |   42                                |         |          |     |
 +   4 +                                   +         +          +     +
     |                                     |         |          |     |
     |   37                                |         |          |     |
 +   3 +                                   +         +          +     +
     |                                     |         |          |     |
     |   11                                |         |          | --- |
     |   12                                |         |          |     |
 +   2 +                                   +         +          +     +
     |   44                                |         |          |     |
     |   32                                |         |          |  4  |
     |   15                                |         |          |     |
 +   1 + 31   36                           +         +          + --- +
     |   8                                 |         | S3       |     |
     |   19   28   29                      |         |          |  3  |
     |   17                                |         | S4   S5  |     |
     |   16   30   5                       | Rater B |          |     |
 *   0 * 13   14   6                        * Rater C *         * --- *
     |   26   38                           | Rater A | S2   S6  |     |
     |   33   39   9                       |         | S7       |  2  |
     |   10   22   34   35   4   41        |         |          |     |
     |   18   27                           |         | S1       |     |
 +  -1 + 1    23   24   40                 +         +          + --- +
     |   21                                |         |          |     |
     |   2                                 |         |          |     |
     |   25   7                            |         |          |  1  |
 +  -2 +                                   +         +          +     +
     |                                     |         |          |     |
     |   3                                 |         |          |     |
     |                                     |         |          | --- |
 +  -3 +                                   +         +          +     +
     |                                     |         |          |     |
     |                                     |         |          |     |
 +  -4 + 20                                +         +          + (0) +

|Measr |+examinees                        |-raters  |-segments |Scale|
```

The global FACETS reports illustrate unified scales of the multi-facets involved in the scoring process of the two criteria, which empower us to measure examinee ability, rater severity, and segment difficulty. With a rough view of the reports, it is able to see that raters are more consistent with severity or leniency when using the PA-based criterion. For more and detailed information, it is discussed in the following sections.

5.3.2.2.2　Unexpected Responses: A Prerequisite for Single-Facet Analysis

Zhang (2017) suggests that researchers, when using FACETS for Rasch analysis, investigate the degree to which the observed scores fit the expected scores that are generated by the model[①]. The unexpected response is a key indicator of fit, which means a situation in which the observed scores misfit the scores estimated in the model. The match, according to Linacre (2005), is characterized with two standards: first, unexpected responses with absolute standardized residuals larger than 2 should account for less than 5% of the total observed scores; second, unexpected responses with absolute standardized residuals larger than 3 should account for less than 1% of the total observed counts. In the study, the PA-based criterion has 924 scores (3 raters, 44 examinees, 7 segments), and the EIC criterion has 924 scores, too. Based on Linacre's standards, if FACETS data are to be judged as fitting the estimates, there should be no more than 47 unexpected responses with absolute standardized residuals of unexpected responses (>2), and there should be no more than 10 unexpected responses with absolute standardized residuals of unexpected responses (>3). Table 5.12, Table 5.13, and Table 5.14 present the unexpected responses of the two criteria.

---

① Expected score, or fair average, fair score, is a score that an examinee could possibly get from a rater of average severity, based on Rasch analysis estimates.

Table 5.12 Unexpected Responses of the PA-Based Criterion

Cat	Step	Exp	Resd	StRes	No. of Raters	Nu	Ex	N	SE
5	5	1.6	3.4	4	1 Rater A	38	38	4	S4
3	3	0.8	2.2	3	3 Rater C	7	7	6	S6
0	0	3.6	−3.6	−3	3 Rater C	37	37	6	S6
5	5	1.9	3.1	3	3 Rater C	40	40	3	S3
5	5	2.0	3.0	3	3 Rater C	40	40	4	S4
5	5	2.0	3.0	3	3 Rater C	40	40	5	S5
2	2	4.5	−2.5	−3	3 Rater C	42	42	6	S6

Table 5.13 Unexpected Responses of the EIC Criterion

Cat	Step	Exp	Resd	StRes	No. of Raters	Nu	Ex	N	SE
3	3	0.1	2.9	9	3 Rater C	20	20	3	S3
4	4	5.0	−1.0	−5	3 Rater C	43	43	2	S2
3	3	4.7	−1.7	−3	1 Rater A	11	11	2	S2
3	3	4.7	−1.7	−3	1 Rater A	11	11	6	S6
1	1	0.1	0.9	3	2 Rater B	20	20	3	S3
3	3	0.6	2.4	3	3 Rater C	3	3	2	S2
3	3	0.7	2.3	−3	3 Rater C	3	3	7	S7
4	4	4.9	−0.9	−3	3 Rater C	42	42	2	S2

Table 5.14 Absolute Standardized Residuals of the Two Criteria

	The PA-Based Criterion	The EIC Criterion
$|StRe|<2$	917	916
$2\leq|StRe|<3$	0	0
$3\leq|StRe|$	7	8
Total Scores	924	924

Table 5.12 shows that for the PA-based criterion, there are 7 unexpected responses with absolute standardized residuals larger than 3, accounting for 0.76% of the total 924 scores. In the case of EIC, unexpected responses are 8, accounting for 0.87% of the total 924 scores. There are no unexpected responses with absolute standardized residuals larger than 2 in both criteria. For the PA-based criterion, 6 out of 7 unexpected responses are from Rater C, which is perhaps a personal issue, implying that Rater C might have been careless, or failed to understand the rules of the criterion, especially when rating examinee No. 40. There are 3 unexpected responses of No.40 scores from Rater C. Another inspiring fact is that unexpected responses incurred by raters appear in last few examinees (NO. 37, NO. 38, No. 40, No. 42), suggesting that raters were less concentrative at the end of rating work, as PA-based rating is labor-intensive. For the EIC criterion, all three raters have some unexpected responses. In Segment 2, in special, there are 4 unexpected responses (50% of all unexpected responses) with absolute standardized residuals above 3, from Rater A and Rater C, indicating they are way too severe or lenient with this segment. The statistical data, based on Linacre's standards, demonstrate that both PA-based scores and EIC-based scores fit MFRM estimates, which are eligible for further in-depth data analysis.

Unexpected response is an indicator of raters' extreme scores, which tells whether the raters over-score or under-score examinees' performance. In this case, unexpected scores with the PA-based criterion and the EIC criterion are close in number, indicating that both criteria are feasible in rating information fidelity. Furthermore, numerous unexpected responses from a certain rater reveals that he/she is either irresponsible, careless or needs further rater training.

5.3.2.2.3 Examining the Examinee Facet

Table 5.15, Table 5.16 and Table 5.17 illustrate examinee measurement reports of the two criteria presented by FACETS. In Table 5.16 and Table 5.17, the first column is the observed scores of examinees from all three raters. The second column is the observed counts (3 raters * 7 segments). The third column is the observed average score of every count, followed by calibrated average score compensated for the model-based inter-rater severity in the fourth column. The column of Measure is a list of examinee ability of information fidelity in interpreting in *logits*, listed from the highest ability to the lowest. The next column, Model SE, means Model Standard Error. The next four columns are Infit MnSq, Infit Zstd, Outfit MnSq and Outfid Zsted respectively (introduced in 5.2). The last two columns are Estimated Discrimination (Estim. Discrm) and the number of examinees.

The author picks out some key indicators from the measurement reports and presents them in Table 5.15, so as to evaluate these two criteria.

Table 5.15 Indicators of Examinee Measurement Reports of the Two Criteria

Indicators	the PA-Based Criterion	the EIC Criterion
Span of Ability	−4.20—6.20	−4.02—4.89
Mean Model SE	0.32	0.31
Separation Ratio	6.56	5.06
Separation Index	9.08	7.08
Reliability of Separation	0.98	0.96
Chi-Square	1,250.5	798.4
Significance (*p*)	0	0
No. of Significant Overfit	3	3
No. of Significant Misfit	0	0

Table 5.16 Examinee Measurement Report of the PA-Based Criterion

Obsvd Score	Obsvd Count	Obsvd Average	Fair-M Average	Measure	Model SE	Infit MnSq	Infit Zstd	Outfit MnSq	Outfit Zstd	Estim. Discrm	Examinees
104	21	5.0	5.01	6.20	0.77	0.45	−0.9	0.20	−0.2	1.33	42
104	21	5.0	5.01	6.20	0.77	0.45	−0.9	0.20	−0.2	1.33	43
100	21	4.8	4.81	4.59	0.53	0.87	−0.1	0.95	0.1	1.02	11
80	21	4.3	4.38	2.92	0.33	1.28	0.8	1.54	1.3	0.35	44
88	21	4.2	4.29	2.71	0.32	0.44	−2.1	0.44	−1.8	1.57	37
79	21	3.8	3.85	1.92	0.29	0.59	−1.5	0.78	−0.6	1.84	12
71	21	3.4	3.39	1.27	0.28	0.52	−1.7	0.53	−1.6	1.56	15
68	21	3.2	3.22	1.03	0.28	0.75	−0.7	0.70	−0.9	1.20	36
62	21	3.0	2.88	0.55	0.28	1.15	0.5	0.97	0	1.10	28
62	21	3.0	2.88	0.55	0.28	1.06	0.2	1.00	0.1	1.04	32
61	21	2.9	2.82	0.48	0.28	0.70	−0.9	0.62	−1.2	1.40	31
58	21	2.8	2.67	0.24	0.28	1.20	0.7	1.07	0.3	0.92	17
58	21	2.8	2.67	0.24	0.28	1.64	1.7	1.51	1.4	0.51	29
56	21	2.7	2.57	0.09	0.28	1.51	1.5	1.51	1.4	0.41	14
56	21	2.7	2.57	0.09	0.28	0.66	−1.1	0.63	−1.1	1.37	19
54	21	2.6	2.47	−0.06	0.28	1.27	0.9	1.24	0.8	0.67	39
53	21	2.5	2.42	−0.14	0.27	0.67	−1.0	0.67	−1.0	0.27	8
49	21	2.3	2.23	−0.44	0.27	0.54	−1.7	0.60	−1.4	1.40	35
48	21	2.3	2.19	−0.51	0.27	2.01	2.6	1.71	2.0	0.38	46
48	21	2.3	2.19	−0.51	0.27	0.42	−2.3	0.47	−2.0	1.59	30
48	21	2.3	2.19	−0.51	0.27	2.91	4.2	3.76	5.6	−1.94	38
47	21	2.2	2.14	−0.58	0.27	0.50	−1.9	0.54	−1.7	1.52	5
44	21	2.1	2.01	−0.81	0.27	0.71	−0.9	0.79	−0.6	1.28	27
42	21	2.0	1.92	−0.95	0.27	1.07	0.3	0.99	0	1.07	22
42	21	2.0	1.92	−0.95	0.27	0.66	−1.2	0.70	−1.0	1.34	26
38	21	1.8	1.75	−1.25	0.27	0.95	0	1.07	0.3	0.86	18
38	21	1.8	1.75	−1.25	0.27	1.43	1.3	1.36	1.2	0.70	33
36	21	1.7	1.66	−1.40	0.28	0.69	−1.0	0.73	−0.9	1.34	24
35	21	1.7	1.62	−1.48	0.28	0.71	−0.9	0.70	−1.0	1.30	6
32	21	1.5	1.49	−1.71	0.28	1.76	2.1	1.61	1.8	0.29	9
31	21	1.5	1.44	−1.79	0.28	1.91	2.4	2.02	2.7	−0.45	21
30	21	1.4	1.40	−1.87	0.29	1.04	0.2	1.17	0.6	0.92	1
29	21	1.4	1.35	−1.96	0.29	0.61	−1.4	0.56	−1.6	1.39	4
29	21	1.4	1.35	−1.96	0.29	0.48	−2.0	0.49	−2.0	1.61	10
29	21	1.4	1.35	−1.96	0.29	0.90	−0.2	1.16	0.6	0.78	41
28	21	1.3	1.31	−2.04	0.29	0.78	−0.6	0.73	−0.8	1.26	34
27	21	1.3	1.26	−2.13	0.29	0.40	−2.4	0.37	−2.6	1.73	2
27	21	1.3	1.26	−2.13	0.29	0.99	0	0.90	−0.2	1.08	40
25	21	1.2	1.18	−2.30	0.30	1.17	0.6	1.03	0.1	1.11	13
25	21	1.2	1.18	−2.30	0.30	0.58	−1.5	1.58	−1.5	1.37	25
24	21	1.1	1.13	−2.39	0.30	0.57	−1.5	0.67	−1.1	1.27	23
15	21	0.7	0.71	−3.33	0.35	0.77	−0.6	0.73	−0.7	1.31	3
13	21	0.6	0.62	−3.59	0.37	1.64	1.7	1.37	1.0	0.74	7
9	21	0.4	0.42	−4.20	0.42	0.44	−1.9	0.41	−1.6	1.66	20

Obsvd Score	Obsvd Count	Obsvd Average	Fair-M Average	Measure	Model SE	Infit MnSq	Infit Zstd	Outfit MnSq	Outfit Zstd	Estim. Discrm	Examinees
48.0	21.0	2.3	2.25	−0.40	0.32	0.95	−0.3	0.95	−0.2	—	Mean (COUNT: 44)
23.6	0	1.1	1.15	2.22	0.11	0.52	1.5	0.59	1.5	—	SD(Populn)
23.9	0	1.1	1.16	2.25	0.11	0.53	1.5	0.60	1.5	—	SD(Sample)

Model, Populn:	RMSE 0.34 Adj (True) SD 2.20 Separation 6.56 Reliability 0.98
Model, Sample:	RMSE 0.34 Adj (True) SD 2.23 Separation 6.64 Reliability 0.98
Model, Fixed (All Same)	Chi-Square: 1,250.5 df: 43 Significance (probability): 0
Model, Random (Normal)	Chi-Square: 40.6 df: 42 Significance (probability): 0.53

Table 5.17 Examinee Measurement Report of the EIC Criterion

Obsvd Score	Obsvd Count	Obsvd Average	Fair-M Average	Measure	Model SE	Infit MnSq	Infit Zstd	Outfit MnSq	Outfit Zstd	Estim. Discrm	Examinees
104	21	5.0	4.96	4.89	0.99	0.98	0.3	1.29	0.6	0.96	43
103	21	4.9	4.92	4.20	0.70	0.92	0.1	0.95	0.2	0.98	42
99	21	4.7	4.75	3.08	0.41	0.63	−0.7	0.66	−0.5	1.08	37
95	21	4.5	4.58	2.54	0.33	1.82	1.9	2.24	2.3	0.44	11
91	21	4.3	4.39	2.15	0.29	0.63	−1.1	0.64	−1.0	1.29	12
85	21	4.0	4.10	1.69	0.26	0.87	−0.3	0.93	−0.1	0.82	44
82	21	3.9	3.95	1.50	0.25	0.94	−0.1	0.90	−0.2	1.10	32
73	21	3.5	3.50	0.98	0.23	0.93	−0.1	0.95	0	1.15	15
72	21	3.4	3.45	0.93	0.23	0.71	−1.0	0.71	−1.0	1.37	31
71	21	3.4	3.40	0.87	0.23	0.59	−1.5	0.60	−1.5	1.52	36
68	21	3.2	3.26	0.72	0.23	0.81	−0.5	0.79	−0.6	1.15	8
64	21	3.0	3.06	0.51	0.22	1.16	0.6	1.14	0.5	0.89	29
63	21	3.0	3.01	0.46	0.22	0.47	−2.2	0.49	−2.1	1.66	19
63	21	3.0	3.01	0.46	0.22	0.78	−0.7	0.78	−0.7	1.17	28
58	21	2.8	2.77	0.22	0.22	1.65	1.9	1.66	2.0	0.14	17
55	21	2.6	2.62	0.07	0.22	0.99	0	0.99	0	1.08	5
54	21	2.6	2.57	0.02	0.22	0.97	0	0.98	0	1.01	16
54	21	2.6	2.57	0.02	0.22	0.45	−2.3	0.44	−2.3	1.65	30
53	21	2.5	2.52	−0.03	0.22	0.37	−2.7	0.37	−2.8	1.79	6
53	21	2.5	2.52	−0.03	0.22	1.46	1.4	1.48	1.5	0.49	14
51	21	2.4	2.42	−0.13	0.22	1.99	2.7	1.97	2.7	−0.06	13
49	21	2.3	2.33	−0.23	0.22	1.00	0.1	0.98	0	0.86	26
46	21	2.2	2.18	−0.38	0.22	0.79	−0.6	0.79	−0.6	1.29	38
45	12	2.1	2.13	−0.43	0.23	1.50	1.5	1.46	1.4	0.28	9
43	21	2.0	2.03	−0.53	0.23	0.74	−0.8	0.75	−0.8	1.32	39
42	21	2.0	1.98	−0.58	0.23	0.78	−0.7	0.78	−0.7	1.12	33
41	21	2.0	1.93	−0.63	0.23	0.39	−2.6	0.38	−2.7	1.79	10
41	21	2.0	1.93	−0.63	0.23	0.98	0	0.98	0	0.99	34
40	21	1.9	1.88	−0.68	0.23	0.56	−1.6	0.55	−1.7	1.61	4
40	21	1.9	1.88	−0.68	0.23	0.93	−0.1	0.87	−0.3	1.20	22
40	21	1.9	1.88	−0.68	0.23	1.21	0.7	1.20	0.7	0.74	41
38	21	1.8	1.78	−0.79	0.23	0.85	−0.4	0.83	−0.5	1.30	35
37	21	1.8	1.73	−0.84	0.23	0.46	−2.2	0.42	−2.4	1.60	27
35	21	1.7	1.63	−0.95	0.24	1.06	0.2	1.04	0.2	0.93	18
33	21	1.6	1.53	−1.07	0.24	0.51	−1.9	0.51	−1.9	1.54	24
33	21	1.6	1.53	−1.07	0.24	0.98	0	0.93	−0.1	1.05	40
32	21	1.5	1.48	−1.12	0.24	1.20	0.7	1.26	0.8	0.78	1
32	21	1.5	1.48	−1.12	0.24	1.08	0.3	1.03	0.2	0.95	23
30	21	1.4	1.39	−1.24	0.25	1.80	2.2	1.65	1.9	−0.01	21
25	21	1.2	1.15	−1.56	0.26	1.02	0.1	1.06	0.2	0.91	2
24	21	1.1	1.10	−1.63	0.26	1.09	0.3	1.04	0.2	0.94	7
23	21	1.1	1.05	1.70	0.27	0.65	−1.1	0.63	−1.2	1.36	25
13	21	0.6	0.58	−2.55	0.33	1.75	1.8	1.64	1.6	0.61	3
4	21	0.2	0.17	−4.02	0.53	2.93	2.7	6.07	4.6	0.25	20

Obsvd Score	Obsvd Count	Obsvd Average	Fair-M Average	Measure	Model SE	Infit MnSq	Infit Zstd	Outfit MnSq	Outfit Zstd	Estim. Discrm	Examinees
52.2	21.0	2.5	2.48	0	0.28	1.01	−0.1	1.09	−0.1	—	Mean (COUNT: 44)
23.7	0	1.1	1.15	1.61	0.14	0.49	1.4	0.86	1.5	—	SD(Populn)
23.9	0	1.1	1.16	1.62	0.14	0.50	1.4	0.87	1.5	—	SD(Sample)

Model, Populn: RMSE 0.31 Adj (True) SD 1.57   Separation 5.06   Reliability 0.96

Model, Sample: RMSE 0.31 Adj (True) SD 1.59   Separation 5.13   Reliability 0.96

Model, Fixed (All Same)   Chi-Square: 798.4   df: 43   Significance (probability): 0

Model, Random (Normal)   Chi-Square: 38.3   df: 42   Significance (probability): 0.64

For starters, examinees differ significantly in terms of their performance in information transfer ($p = 0 < 0.05$), which means that both criteria are capable of separating examinees' ability in this regard. For the Mean Model Standard Error (SE), the PA-based criterion (0.32) is almost the same as the EIC criterion (0.31). Separation Ratio of the PA-based criterion is a bit higher than that of the EIC criterion, implying a better capability of differentiating examinee ability in information transfer (6.56 vs. 5.06). Separation indices of the two criteria (9.08 vs. 7.08) mean that PA-based criterion classifies examinee ability into 9 strata, and the EIC criterion classifies the ability into 7 strata. Both criteria have reached a high level of reliability in terms of separation index (0.98 and 0.96). Chi-square data show that the PA-based criterion (1,250.5) is higher than the EIC criterion (798.4). These indicators demonstrate that both criteria are reliable in assessing examinees ability of information fidelity. These two criteria have their advantages in this aspect, albeit insignificant ones.

From the perspective of fit indices, observed scores are similar in fitting the model. McNamara (1996) suggests that fit index, based on Infit MnSq, range between (Mean− 2*SD, Mean+ 2*SD). Based on the suggestion, the reasonable fluctuations of Infit MnSq for the PA-based criterion and the EIC criterion should be −0.36 to 2.32 and −0.03 to 1.99 respectively. For a PA-based score, if its Infit MnSq value is more than 2.32, then it overfits with the model; if its Infit MnSq value is lower than −0.36, then it misfits with the model. For EIC scores, the Infit MnSq value higher than 1.99 means overfit, and the value lower than −0.03 means misfit. From Table 5.16 and Table 5.17, there is no misfit for both criteria. And there are 3 overfit instances for both criteria.

To summarize, as to the examinee facet, both the PA-based criterion and the EIC criterion are capable of stratifying examinee competence in message transfer, and categorizing it into various strata with high reliability. Each criterion has its merits, for instance, the PA-based criterion may lead to less discrepancies among raters, while the EIC criterion are better in differentiating examinee ability. In addition, statistics show that scores based on the two criteria fit the MFRM analysis estimates.

5.3.2.2.4 Examining the Rater Facet

Measurement reports of the rater facet are shown in Table 5.18 and Table 5.19.

Table 5.18 Rater Measurement Report of the PA-Based Criterion

Obsvd Score	Obsvd Count	Obsvd Average	Fair-M Average	Measure	Model SE	Infit		Outfit		Exact Obsv. (%)	Agree Obsv. (%)	No. of Raters
						MnSq	Zstd	MnSq	Zstd			
698	308	2.3	2.10	0.02	0.06	0.80	−2.6	0.80	−2.5	59.6	34.0	2 Rater B
704	308	2.3	2.12	−0.01	0.06	0.86	−1.8	0.86	−1.6	55.7	33.9	1 Rater A
705	308	2.3	2.12	−0.01	0.06	1.29	3.2	1.31	3.3	52.3	33.9	3 Rater C
Model, Populn: RMSE 0.06 Adj (True) SD 0 Separation 0 Reliability 0												
Model, Sample: RMSE 0.06 Adj (True) SD 0 Separation 0 Reliability 0												
Model, Fixed (all same) Chi-Square: 0.1 df: 2 Significance (probability): 0.95												
Model, Random (normal) Chi-Square: 0.1 df: 1 Significance (probability): 0.74												
Rater agreement opportunities: 924 Exact agreements: 516 = 55.8% Expected: 313.7 = 34.0%												

Table 5.19 Rater Measurement Report of the EIC Criterion

Obsvd Score	Obsvd Count	Obsvd Average	Fair-M Average	Measure	Model SE	Infit		Outfit		Exact Obsv. (%)	Agree Obsv. (%)	No. of Raters
						MnSq	Zstd	MnSq	Zstd			
711	308	2.3	2.33	0.22	0.06	0.86	−1.8	0.82	−1.9	49.8	34.8	2 Rater B
747	308	2.4	2.48	0.08	0.06	1.00	0	1.40	3.6	43.7	35.2	1 Rater C
839	308	2.7	2.85	−0.30	0.06	1.03	0.4	1.04	0.4	43.5	34.5	3 Rater A
Model, Populn: RMSE 0.06 Adj (True) SD 0.21 Separation 3.28 Reliability 0.91												
Model, Sample: RMSE 0.06 Adj (True) SD 0.26 Separation 4.08 Reliability 0.94												
Model, Fixed (all same) Chi-Square: 35.4 df: 2 Significance (probability): 0.00												
Model, Random (normal) Chi-Square: 1.9 df: 1 Significance (probability): 0.17												
Rater agreement opportunities: 924 Exact agreements: 516 = 45.7% Expected: 313.7 = 34.8%												

The first four columns are the total Observed Scores, Observed Counts, Observed Average Score and Fair-Mean Average Sore. Then the two columns to the right represent Mearsure and Standard Error on the measurement scale; the higher the value is, the severer the rater is. Similar to the report of examinees, the last six columns stand for Infit MnSq, Infit Zstd, Outfit MnSq, Outfit Zstd, Exact and Agree Estimated Discrimination, and the No. of Raters. Table 5.20 presents some key indicators of the facet.

Table 5.20   Indicators of Rater Measurement Report of the Two Criteria

Indicators	The PA-Based Criterion	The EIC Criterion
Span of Severity	−0.10—0.02	−0.30—0.22
Mean Model SE	0.06	0.06
Separation Ratio	0	3.28
Separation Index	0	4.69
Reliability of Separation	0	0.91
Chi-Square	0.1	35.4
Significance (p)	0.95	0
Exact Obs (%)	55.9	45.6
No. of Significant Misfit	0	0
No. of Significant Overfit	0	0

These indicators mainly represent rater severity and inter-rater reliability. Raters with the PA-based criterion have maintained a very high homogeneity (−0.10, 0.02, −0.01 respectively). It means that three raters have reached a high degree of agreement with the PA-based criterion. Raters with the EIC criterion also manage to reach agreement (−0.30, 0.22, 0.08), which show the severity of the EIC criterion is a bit more fluctuative than that of the PA-based criterion.

Rater severity alone cannot reveal too much information, without detecting interaction facet. A merit of Rasch analysis is that it could connect the inter-related facets. If we can measure rater severity with examinee ability, then it is possible to understand to what degree rater severity affects scoring results. Myford & Wolfe (2000) propose a formulation to calculate the impact of rater severity on score.

$$z = \frac{RS - rs}{EA - ea} \times 100\%$$

z = probability of the impact of rater severity on examinee score;

RS = maximum rater severity;

rs = minimum rater severity;

EA = maximum examinee ability;

ea = minimum examinee ability.

Based on this equation, it is possible to know the degree that rater severity affects examinee score with the two criteria. First, for the PA-based criterion, z = (0.02+0.10)/(6.20+4.20) × 100% = 1.2%; for the EIC criterion, z = (0.22+0.30)/(4.89+4.02) × 100% = 5.8%. The ratio means that when an examinee is assessed by a rater using the PA-based criterion, there is a probability of 0.5% that his score is affected by the criterion. For the EIC criterion, the probability is 5.8%. Data reiterate that both criteria are capable of assessing examinee ability of message transfer, but the PA-based criterion is a bit more reliable, less likely to be affected by rater bias.

Further, with other indicators, the PA-based criterion has also proved to be reliable. Statistical data show that there is no significant difference among raters (Separation Ratio = 0; Separation Index = 0; Reliability = 0; Chi-square = 0.1; p = 0.95). It is also shown that the EIC criterion is reliable, only a bit higher than PA (Separation Ratio = 3.28; Separation Index = 4.69; Reliability = 0.91; Chi-square = 35.4). What deserves our attention is that p= 0<0.05, meaning that rater severity is significantly heterogeneous. Also, Separation index of the PA-based criterion is 0, which implies that three raters with the PA-based criterion have maintained high consistency in scoring severity. Separation Index of the

EIC criterion is 4.69, meaning that rater severity could be stratified into 5 levels.

The last indicator to be discussed here is Exact Obs(%), which is another index of inter-rater consistency, ranging between 0—100%. The closer the Exact Obs(%) gets to 100%, the more homogenous raters are in scoring results and the more instances that raters' ratings are exactly fitting the Model estimates. Exact Obs(%) of PA is 55.9%, 10 percentage higher than 45.6% of EIC.

Evidence collected from the rater facet points to the fact that the raters could not reach to agreement occasionally when using the EIC criterion, compared to the PA-based criterion, which coincides with the results of inter-rater reliability investigation with SPSS analysis. Both statistical means lead to the same conclusion that raters with the PA-based criterion are more likely to achieve higher inter-rater agreement.

5.3.2.2.5 Examining the Difficulty Facet

In addition to examinees' ability of the message transfer and rater severity, FACETS can also analyze item/task difficulty. In this section, Rasch analysis of the facet of segment is presented, so as to understand segmental difficulty. Data of the facet are presented in Table 5.21 and Table 5.22.

Table 5.21 Segment Measurement Report of the PA-Based Criterion

Obsvd Score	Obsvd Count	Obsvd Average	Fair-M Avrage	Measure	Model SE	Infit MnSq	Infit Zstd	Outfit MnSq	Outfit Zstd	Estim. Discrm	Nu	Segments
240	132	1.8	1.67	0.61	0.09	0.70	−2.6	0.66	−2.8	1.35	5	S5
229	132	1.7	1.51	0.48	0.11	1.04	0.3	1.09	0.6	0.93	3	S3
245	132	1.9	1.63	0.44	0.10	1.05	0.4	1.12	0.8	0.97	4	S4
309	132	2.3	2.26	−0.06	0.11	0.96	−0.3	0.95	−0.3	1.02	2	S2
342	132	2.6	2.52	−0.26	0.09	1.12	0.9	1.16	1.2	0.87	6	S6
375	132	2.8	2.77	−0.57	0.09	1.16	1.2	1.08	0.6	0.91	7	S7
367	132	2.8	2.73	−0.64	0.10	0.87	−1.0	0.85	−1.2	1.12	1	S1

Continued

Obsvd Score	Obsvd Count	Obsvd Average	Fair-M Avrage	Measure	Model SE	Infit MnSq	Infit Zstd	Outfit MnSq	Outfit Zstd	Estim. Discrm	Nu	Segments
301.0	132	2.3	2.16	0	0.10	0.99	−0.1	0.99	−0.1	—		Mean (Count: 7)
58.1	0	0.4	0.51	0.48	0.01	0.14	1.2	0.17	1.3	—		SD(Populn)
62.1	0	0.5	0.55	0.52	0.01	0.16	1.3	0.18	1.4	—		SD(Sample)

Model, Populn: RMSE 0.10 Adj (True) SD 0.47 Separation 4.71 Reliability 0.96

Model, Sample: RMSE 0.10 Adj (True) SD 0.51 Separation 5.11 Reliability 0.96

Model, Fixed (all same) Chi-Square: 169.9 df: 6 Significance (probability): 0

Model, Random (normal) Chi-Square: 5.8 df: 5 Significance (probability): 0.33

Table 5.22 Segment Measurement Report of the EIC Criterion

Obsvd Score	Obsvd Count	Obsvd Average	Fair-M Average	Measure	Model SE	Infit MnSq	Infit Zstd	Outfit MnSq	Outfit Zstd	Estim. Discrm	Nu	Segments
253	132	1.9	1.85	0.72	0.10	0.85	−1.2	1.70	4.2	0.94	3	S3
275	132	2.1	2.06	0.50	0.10	0.73	−2.3	0.68	−2.5	1.34	4	S4
279	132	2.1	2.10	0.46	0.10	0.98	−0.1	0.90	−0.6	1.07	5	S5
346	132	2.6	2.73	−0.17	0.10	1.27	2.0	1.23	1.4	0.76	6	S6
351	132	2.7	2.77	−0.22	0.10	0.93	−0.5	1.28	1.7	0.90	2	S2
371	132	2.8	2.95	−0.40	0.10	0.81	−1.5	0.79	−1.3	1.22	7	S7
422	132	3.2	3.41	−0.88	0.10	1.16	1.2	1.06	0.3	0.89	1	S1
328.1	132	2.5	2.55	0	0.10	0.96	−0.4	1.09	0.4	—		Mean (Count: 7)
56.5	0	0.4	0.52	0.53	0	0.18	1.5	0.32	2.1	—		SD(Populn)
61.1	0	0.5	0.57	0.58	0	0.19	1.6	0.35	2.3	—		SD(Sample)

Model, Populn: RMSE 0.10 Adj (True) SD 0.53 Separation 5.36 Reliability 0.97

Model, Sample: RMSE 0.10 Adj (True) SD 0.57 Separation 5.80 Reliability 0.97

Model, Fixed (all same) Chi-Square: 204.6 df: 6 Significance (probability): 0

Model, Random (normal) Chi-Square: 5.8 df: 5 Significance (probability): 0.32

The first four columns stand for Observed Scores, Observed Counts, Observed Average score and Fair-Mean Average Score of each segment, followed by Measure (segment difficulty) and MFRM Standard Error. Generally speaking, higher value of the Measure means higher segmental difficulty. Infit and Outfit MnSq represent the degree that the Observed Score fits the model. The last two columns are Estimated Discrimination and Number of Segment. Key indicators of the facet are presented and compared in Table 5.23.

Table 5.23 Indicators of Segment Measurement Report of the Two Criteria

Indicators	the PA-Based Criterion	the EIC Criterion
Span of Segment Diff.	−0.64—0.61	−0.88—0.72
Mean Model SE	0.10	0.10
Separation Ratio	4.71	5.36
Separation Index	6	7
Reliability of Separation	0.96	0.97
Chi-Square	169.9	204.6
Significance (p)	0.00	0.00
No. of Significant Misfit	0	0
No. of Significant Overfit	0	0

With the help of some key indicators, it is possible to tell segment difficulty and whether the two criteria can measure segment difficulty against examinee ability, in terms of information fidelity in interpreting test.

First, data reveal the number of significant misfits and overfits. It has been discussed that fit could fluctuate between (Mean Infit MnSq -2S.D., Mean Infit MnSq +2S.D.). Thus, the PA-based criterion's infit range is 0.72—1.27, segement with Infit MnSq above 1.27 is considered as overfit, and Infit MnSq below 0.72 is misfit. The EIC criterion's fit range is 0.6—1.32. There is no sign of misfit and overfit in either criterion, impling that both criteria can measure segment difficulty properly.

Second, indicators of the two criteria show clear differentiation among segments (p: 0 vs. 0, separation ration: 4.71 vs. 5.36, reliability of separation index: 0.96 vs. 0.97). These data point out that raters can properly assess examinee performance segmentally; there is neither halo effect nor central tendancy in scoring process. (Eckes, 2015)

Seen from the data of segment facet, the two criteria under investigation are capable of measuring segment difficulty against examinee ability, in terms of information fidelity.

5.3.2.2.6 Examining Rater Bias

Previously, facets of examinee ability, rater severity and segment difficulty are analyzed respectively. In this part, the author is going to discuss interaction facet, namely, interaction between raters and examinee ability.

Interaction analysis, or bias analysis, refers to the possibility of examinee scores affected by rater severity. If a rater is too severe or lenient in rating, it is likely to result in extreme scores. FACETS can analyze and sort out extreme scores that do not fit the Model estimates. The percentage of these extreme scores is an important indicator to evaluate criterion appropriacy. Table 5.24 and Table 5.25 list the extreme scores in the PA-based criterion and the EIC criterion.

Table 5.24 Rater Bias of the PA-Based Criterion

Obsvd Score	Exp Score	Obsvd Count	Obs-Exp Average	Bias Size	Model SE	t	Infit MnSq	Outfit MnSq	Sq	No of Raters	Measr	Ex	Measr
25.0	20.8	7.0	0.60	1.00	0.49	2.04	0.8	0.8	96	3 Rater C	−0.04	32	0.55
16.0	16.0	7.0	0	0.01	0.55	0	0.9	0.9		Mean(Count: 132)			
8.0	7.9	0	0.17	0.36	0.20	0.61	0.7	0.7		SD(Populn)			
8.0	7.9	0	0.17	0.37	0.20	0.61	0.7	0.7		SD(Sample)			
Fixed (all = 0) Chi-square: 48.4 df: 132 Significance (probability): 1.00													

Note: Bias/Interaction analysis specified by: raters; examinees

Table 5.25 Rater Bias of the EIC Criterion

Obsvd Score	Exp Score	Obsvd Count	Obs-Exp Average	Bias Size	Model SE	t	Infit MnSq	Outfit MnSq	Sq	No. of Raters	Measr	Ex	Measr
31	18.9	7	1.73	2.53	0.61	4.13	0.5	0.4	37	1 Rater A	−0.38	13	−0.25
9	4.0	7	0.71	1.10	0.41	2.66	1.3	1.3	9	3 Rater C	0.01	3	−2.55
23	18.0	7	0.72	0.86	0.42	2.06	0.7	0.6	50	2 Rater B	0.17	17	0.14
13	7.9	7	0.74	0.84	0.39	2.15	0.6	0.6	6	3 Rater C	0.01	2	−1.65
15	21.2	7	−0.88	−1.03	0.40	−2.58	2.2	2.3	49	1 Rater A	−0.38	17	0.14
8	15.6	7	−1.08	−1.22	0.43	−2.85	0.3	0.3	38	2 Rater B	0.17	13	−0.25
11	19.6	7	−1.22	−1.37	0.40	−3.45	0.5	0.3	40	1 Rater A	−0.38	14	−0.14
26	32.3	7	−0.90	−1.87	0.44	−4.24	1.3	1.4	31	1 Rater A	−0.38	11	2.87
17.4	17.4	7.0	0	0.01	0.52	−0.02	0.8	0.7		Mean(Count: 132)			
8.5	8.0	0	0.39	0.67	0.31	1.18	0.5	0.5		SD(Populn)			
8.5	8.0	0	0.40	0.68	0.31	1.18	0.5	0.5		SD(Sample)			
Fixed (all = 0); Chi-Square: 183.7; df: 132; Significance (probability): 0													

Note: Bias/Interaction analysis specified by: raters; examinees

For the EIC criterion, the number of significantly biased scores is 8, accounting for 6% of all 924 scores. This means that rater severity affects examinee scores to a minor extent. And for the EIC criterion, all the three raters have a few cases of significantly biased scores. Rater A, in special, is too severe that some examinees (No. 17, No. 14 , and No. 11) are rated with scores much lower than the Rasch Model estimates (15 vs. 21.2, 11 vs. 19.6, 26 vs. 32.3). For Rater A, B, C, they both exert leniency in rating for one or two examinees' performance, which are all sorted out in Rasch analysis.

There are some new findings when we put the EIC rater measurement report (Table 5.19) and the EIC bias analysis report (Table 5.25) together for analysis.

① For the EIC criterion, Rater Severity/Leniency is a major factor in causing misfitting between Observed Scores and model estimates ($|Ztsd| > 2$ in Table 5.16). Table 5.25 shows that Examinee No.17 and No.13 have experienced rater severity/ leniency twice, which causes them to be on the list of misfit with model. Even though No. 3, No. 14, No. 2 and No. 11 are not on the list, their |Ztsd| are on the verge of the threshhold. This means that the misfit scores are directly caused by significant rater bias. (He & Zhang, 2008; Zhang, 2017).

② For the EIC criterion, rater bias mostly exists among intermediate level examinees. Examinee ability ranges from −4.02 *logits* to 4.20 *logits* (cf. Table 5.17), and most examinees who encount significant rater bias have their ability ranging from −2.55 *logits* to 2.87 *logits*. It seems that raters find it hard to measure intermediate level examinees occasionally. When it occurs, it is likely to cause controversy or discrepancy in scores.

.To sum up, in terms of bias/interaction between rater severity and examinee ability, scores based on the PA-based criterion are much less affected by rater bias than the EIC criterion. There is only one significantly bias-affected score with the PA-based criterion. The number with the EIC criterion is 8. This implies that the raters working with the EIC criterion occasionally score too severely or leniently, which directly causes significantly biased scores. Another major finding of the interaction analysis between raters and examinees is that in the assessment of information fidelity in interpreting, significant rater bias is more likely to fall upon intermediate-level exmaminees, which is also a sign of rater inconsistency and disagreement.

5.3.2.2.7 Summary of FACETS Analysis

On the basis of MFRM analysis, statistical analysis with FACETS has offered some implications for the two criteria under investigation:

① Both criteria bascially fit the MFRM estimates, whether in global or individual terms. This could be seen from the frequencies of raters' unexpected responses of the two criteria. A majority of unexpected responses of the PA-based criterion have been incurred by a given rater, seemingly showing that the PA-based criterion, relative to the EIC criterion, is not easy to control and command. If so, extreme scores or unexpected responses are likely to occur. It is suggested that when using the PA-based criterion, training process be required. Pilot rating should be offered beforehand, ensuring inter-rater and intra-rater reliability.

② As to the facet of examinees, data reveal that the PA-based criterion can better distinguish examinee ability in message rendition in interpreting, in comparison with the EIC criterion.

③ As to the facet of raters, both criteria have obtained high inter-rater consistency. There is no sign of central tendency or halo effect in scoring. Despite that, raters with the PA-based criterion are more likely to achieve inter-rater agreement than with the EIC criterion. That is, raters are more homogeneous when they are with the PA-based criterion.

④ As far as segment difficulty is concerned, scoring data with the two criteria show that the seven segments are appropriately designed. With a relatively fixed segment difficulty in information rendition, interpreting tests can elicit examinee performance which, to a large extent, is a genuine display of their interpreter competence.

⑤ Bias analysis between raters and exminees demonstrates that raters with the PA-based criterion are less intrusive during the process of scoring. In other words, scoring behavior with the PA-based criterion is less influenced by rater bias, indicating feasibility in the assessment of information fidelity.

Generally speaking, Rasch analysis reveals that both criteria have reached satisfacotry inter-rater and intra-rater reliability. They are capable of assessing competence of message rendition, although in certain aspects, the PA-based criterion possesses some advantages over the EIC criterion. These findings are discussed in detail in the next section.

5.4 Discussion

Previously, data analysis by means of SPSS and FACETS is discussed, in an attempt to collect evidence for the validation of the PA-based criterion in the assessment of information fidelity. In this section, discussion centers around findings of the experiment.

5.4.1 Criterion Validity

Criterion validity refers to the extent to which a measure is related to an outcome. Criterion validity consists of concurrent and predictive validity. Concurrent validity refers to a comparison between the proposed measure and an outcome assessed at the same time. Predictive validity, on the other side, refers to a comparsion between the measure in question and an outcome assessed at a later time. In the experiment, the PA-based criterion is proposed, whose validation procedure, from a criterion-validity perspective, is actually to measure its concurrent validity.

The EIC criterion is currently in use in EIC tests, as a reference measure against the PA-based criterion. Data show that the EIC scoring results and the PA scoring results are highly correlated (p = 0.921 > 0.05). The indicator reveals that EIC scores and PA scores are interchangeable. In that sense, the PA-based criterion is validated in terms of concurrent validity. The logic behind it is that if the EIC criterion in current use is valid, the PA-based criterion should also be valid. The EIC criterion for information transfer is a system of weighted scores of segmental information fidelity. Rather than assessing information on the lexical basis, the EIC criterion measures information on the segmental basis, which allows raters to assess information fidelity in a broader context. The practice represents the notions of deverbalisation and meaning-focused assessment of interpreting performance. When using the EIC criterion, raters realize that they could assess information quality on a segmental scale, instead of focusing on minor or trivial additions or omissions of words or phrases. With that said, it is fair to say that the EIC criterion for message transfer is designed on the basis of a theoretical assumption that the major task of interpreting is to render faithfully the author's intended message, rather than lexical meaning, in source language into the target language (Pöchhacker, 2016). In this sense, if the EIC criterion is considered to be valid, the PA-based criterion, highly correlated to the EIC criterion, is also criterion-valid.

5.4.2 Rating Validity/Rater Reliability

Rating validity (Zhang, 2017), or rater reliability, refers to the degree to which "raters can consistently apply the scale/ criterion to rating" (Knoch & Chapelle, 2017: 7). Rater reliability is "a necessary condition for achieving validity" (Han, 2016: 4), apart from construct validity and criterion validity. Indicators of the degree of rater reliability are rater reliability estimates (RREs). RREs could be measured through statistical analysis indicating "rater consistency (e. g., using techniques such as reliability analysis in Classical Test Theory or mean square statistics in many-faceted Rasch analysis)" (Knoch & Chapelle, 2017: 7).

In CTT, RREs are measured in terms of inter-rater reliability coefficient [Kendall's $W(K)^a$] in SPSS analysis. Of the two criteria applied to the assessment of information fidelity in the current investigation, the inter-rater reliability coefficients (IRRs) of PA and EIC are 0.971 and 0.917 respectively. Both criteria achieve high IRRs, implying that raters could well understand the two criteria and use them in scoring. Seen from the seven segments of the speech, both criteria also achieve high IRRs. However, segmental IRRs of PA are all higher than those of EIC, indicating a better rating performance and higher rater consistency. IRRs of PA are all above 0.900 in the seven segments, while only one IRR of EIC is above 0.900, and the rest segmental IRRs range between

0.800 and 0.857. From the perspective of CTT, a correlation efficient (p) of 0.7 is considered that raters' scoring is reliable, and a correlation efficient (p) of 0.9 is "where we might start to feel comfortable that two markers are rating in a similar fashion" (Weir, 2005: 34). Thus, IRRs show that PA-based scores are more reliable than EIC scores, in that PA raters are more likely to achieve rating agreement.

When using the EIC criterion, the raters do not achieve such a high agreement, partly because of the rater training procedure (cf. Section 4.4.2). During the training session for the EIC criterion, a "minimum training" is carried out. Raters listen to anchored recordings, and they are told that the recordings are considered as perfect performance, good performance, less-good performance and bad performance in information fidelity, but the exact scores of those recordings are hidden. Due to different perceptions of information fidelity, different raters would assign different scores to the same recordings, on the basis of their expertise, experiences and personal bias. Besides, raters will inevitably affected by other factors, such as fluency and delivery, as EIC assessment is listening-based. Although raters are reminded to ignore fluency and delivery of the recordings during assessment, it is hard to fully eliminate the "halo effect" of these factors, which finally result in lower IRRs. This issue does not concern PA rating. PA is text-based assessment, completely free from being affected by other factors. This is actually an advantage of analytical assessment. "In case of an analytic scale, scale criteria can be shown to be assessing separate abilities as hypothesized" (Knotch & Chapelle, 2017: 7). It seems that during analytical assessment of interpreting performance, in order to completely free raters from being affected by other factors, the assessment of information fidelity could be text-based. However, this raises another concern. Interpreting performance is complex, and assessment should not be absolutely componential, or it is likely to incur serious consequences. For instance, if an examinee performs very well in information transfer, but poorly in fluency and delivery, should the examinee get a high score? This issue deserves further research, especially when it comes to machine assessment. Nevertheless, it is undeniable that the PA-based criterion is more feasible in the assessment of information fidelity in consecutive interpreting, which coincides with Yeh (2015), with IRR also as high as 0.957.

Correlation analysis in CTT reveals information of rating behavior, considering raters as a whole group. Rasch analysis then reveals information of scoring behavior of raters as independent selves, demonstrating discrepancy among individual raters, including inter-rater consistency, intra-rater consistency and severity/leniency and personal bias exerted in scoring behavior. Such kind of information also serves the validation of the PA-based criterion in this study.

A first Rasch-based indicator of IRR is an unexpected response/extreme score of the PA-based and the EIC criteria. Unexpected response is a result of misfit between the raw/observed scores by raters and the estimated scores by the Rasch Model. The two criteria are close in number of unexpected responses. An interesting finding of the PA-based criterion in this aspect is that of all the 7 unexpected responses, 6 are from Rater C, which means that Rater C has committed a vast majority of deviations in scoring with PA. The most-affected examinee is No.40. Of the seven segments in his performance, score deviations have been found in three segments. Besides, unexpected responses concentrate on NO.37 and No.42. To find out the reasons of unusual frequency of unexpected responses, a post-assessment interview with Rater C is conducted. According to Rater C, score deviations are due to carelessness and physical exhaustion. After the inteview, Rater C re-assesses the three examinees' performance, whose results fit the Model estimates.[1] Apart from 6 unexpected responses from Rater

---

[1] Eckes (2015) recommends that if a rater's scoring behavior is found to deviate from the Rasch Model estimates too much or too many times, the rater's scores should be removed from the database, or the rater should conduct a re-assessment. In the present study, score deviations with PA are due to personal issues, rather than incompetence. Therefore, he is asked to reassess the three examinees' performance.

C, the only unexpected response is from Rater A, referring that the raters could understand the rules of PA and apply them into scoring task consistently. On the other hand, proposition has proved to be a feasible tool and a standardized unit in the assessment of information fidelity.

There are 8 unexpected responses for the EIC criterion. Though these account for a small percentage of all 924 scores, these unexpected responses are found in all three raters' scoring. This could also be explained partially with "minimum training". Rather than stipulating standardized procedure for assessment, the training leaves much room for the raters to make a full play of their personal understanding of information fidelity. This reminds us that for high-stakes interpreting performance tests, training procedure should be strictly stipulated and raters' perceptions of assessment criterion and scale be standardized.

The second indicator of IRR based on Rasch analysis is rater severity (cf. Table 5.18 and Table 5.19). Data show that the three raters are slightly more consistent in severity/leniency when using the PA-based criterion than when they are using the EIC criterion (rater severity with PA ranges between −0.10 and 0.02, severity with EIC ranges between −0.30 and 0.22). But in terms of exact agreements, there are 516 observed scores (55.8% of all 924 scores) under PA and 422 observed scores (45.7% of all 924 scores) under the EIC criterion. Besides, the separation index of rater severity under PA is 0, while that of EIC is 4.69. This means that rater severity of PA does not exist significant discrepancy, whereas rater severity of EIC can be classified into nearly 5 strata, indicating that the three raters are inconsistent with their severity/leniency throughout the scoring process, whose scoring behaviors are occasionally featured with over-severity or over-leniency. It is fair to say that PA, with standardized assessment procedure, is more accurate in assessment scores than EIC. It is also because of a lack of standardized assessment procedure and a unit that raters working with EIC cannot achieve such a high consistency of severity/leniency.

The third indicator of IRR is rater bias, which refers to the degree to which the observed score is affected by rater bias/preference. Similar to the situation of unexpected responses, there is only one instance of significant rater bias for the PA-based criterion, but 8 instances of significant rater bias for the EIC criterion. It implies that PA has the potential to minimize rater bias during scoring behavior, an ideal goal of assessment designers, which could attribute to its strict rules in identifying and classifying propositional correspondence.

Analyzing the data of EIC assessment, it is discovered that intermediate-level examinees are affected by rater bias. Examinee ability ranges from −3.98 *logits* to 6.07 *logits* (see Table 5.13), and for those examinees who encounter significicnat rater bias, their competence of message transfer rangs from −2.55 *logits* to 2.87 *logits*. It seems that the raters find it hard to measure intermediate level examinees from time to time. In this situation, it is likely to cause controversy or discrepancy in scores. This finding is opposite to Zhang (2012) and Zhang (2017), who claim that raters always bias for/against high-level and low-level examinees, while for intermediate-level examinees, they are likely to achieve inter-rater agreement. One reason for these different conclusions may be that this study investigates information fidelity in consecutive interpreting alone; raters could assess examinees' performance dependent on how they render the intended message correctly, completely ignorant of their performance in delivery, grammar, idiomaticity, etc. Thus, when examinees render the message completely and accurately, raters tend to give high scores; when examinees render nothing, or blabber out nonsense, raters will give nothing. The intermediate-level examinees' performance seem to be subject to disagreement in rating. In this scenario, rater bias arises.

To sum up, all the key CTT-based and Rasch-based IRR indicators lead to the conclusion that the PA-based criterion is more likely to achieve inter-rater consistency and intra-rater consistency. Whether working as a group or as individual selves, raters working with PA can fulfill scoring tasks more reliably, with their scores representing examinees' ability more accurately. PA can assure of the minimum effect of rater bias. These high IRRs are mostly due to the standardized assessment procedure of PA.

5.4.3 Rater Training

Rater training is a prerequisite for rater reliability, which is aimed at improving the quality of scoring behavior. Well-designed rater training could ensure consistent scoring behavior among individual raters and rater groups. In this study, two training sessions are organized for raters, one about the PA-based criterion and the other about the EIC criterion. There are some findings about training programs in this investigation, which are presented below.

Fine-grained training session could, to some extent, reduce rating errors and mitigate rater effects. SPSS and Rasch analysis show that raters, using both criteria, behave consistently during scoring tasks. Difference lies in that raters, when working with the PA-based criterion, display higher consistency and inter-rater and intra-rater reliability than that when they are with the EIC criterion. This could partly due to different training sessions, apart from the reason that the PA-based, as a feasible assessment criterion, offers a standard information assessment unit and assessment procedure. The PA training session runs through a procedure of introduction to proposition, propositional correspondence, propositional correspondence relations, identification and classification of PC and pilot assessment, including discussions and Q&A. During the session, the concepts of proposition and PA are introduced in detail. The training session does not move on to the next part, until every rater is sure that everything makes sense. In addition, pilot assessment and the following discussion enable raters to turn the theoretical knowledge of PA into practicable knowledge and regulate their assessment behavior. These measures guarantee that raters command and practice PA in their work efficiently. In this sense, PA empowers raters to detect, identify and classify information fidelity by means of propositional correspondence. Hence, PA has the potential to mitigate error-prone subjectivity in scoring behavior and enhance rating reliability.

In contrast, EIC training session is carried out in a spirit of "minimum training". That is, the assessment scale, assessment sheet and weighted scores are introduced to the raters, followed by pilot assessment of anchored recordings. The trainer reminds the raters frequently that they are supposed to assess information fidelity only. "Minimum training" is not meant to make the EIC criterion fuzzy. As a matter of fact, due to lacking standard information assessment unit, it is very difficult to accurately define information fidelity to the raters. Besides, raters themselves would have different perceptions of information fidelity. The reason of "minimum training" is to make sure that every rater could score examinees' performance consistently, regardless of various perceptions of information fidelity that might lead to inter-rater discrepancy. Results do show that the raters, when working with the EIC criterion, occasionally reach disagreement, which demonstrates different understandings of information fidelity. To minimize disagreement, Rasch analysis could be deployed in pilot assessment to find out the misfitting raters and retrain them to improve their rating accuracy. (Han, 2015; Li & Guan, 2016) For those misfitting raters who are detected after scoring task, it is suggested Post-hoc interviews be conducted and their work be examined, so as to figure out causes of inconsistency (Han, 2016), which could provide clues and suggestions for the refinement of future training programs.

Rater training has proved to be effective in various test assessments (Li & Guan, 2016; Guan, 2014; Guan, etc. 2011; Yang, 2011) but rarely in interpreting tests. The present investigation, though it does not target rater training directly, offers empirical evidence to tell that well-designed rater training could guarantee a satisfactory and reliable scoring result. This issue is of importance for high-stakes tests, especially interpreting performance tests. For the assessment of information fidelity, the issue of whether "sufficient training" or "minimum training" should be adopted deserves our further attention.

5.4.4 Advantages and Disadvantages of PA in the Assessment of Information Fidelity

The experiment adopts PA in assessing examinees' performance in the message transfer, which is measured against the EIC criterion. During the process of validation, some advantages of PA have been detected, together with some disadvantages.

Firstly, proposition, serving as a basic information assessment unit, could detect and measure the message transfer in interpreting performance more accurately. Being a unit of meaning representation in semantics, proposition is naturally appropriate to serve as an information assessment unit. In addition, propositionalization of the source text and the interpreted text is actually a process of message extraction from the surface lexico-grammatical level, which enables raters to focus on information equivalence that transcends lexical assessment. Furthermore, messages in interpreting products are broken down into propositions, which facilitates raters' assessment when they need to rate information fidelity. Based on propositions, raters are more confident and accurate in information assessment, as they focus on one proposition at a time, rather than considering information equivalence at segmental level, which easily lends itself to rater expertise and perceptions of information fidelity. It is reinforced by the data of the experiment, indicating that the PA-based criterion could achieve higher rater consistency and inter-rater and intra-rater reliability than the EIC criterion. In this sense, it leads to a conclusion that for the information assessment in consecutive interpreting, something is better than nothing. A criterion taking proposition as an assessment unit can assess information fidelity more reliably than those criteria with no assessment unit, or with a unit that is vaguely defined, or rater-dependent.

Secondly, PA, by offering a standardized message transfer detection and classification procedure, could facilitate raters in achieving higher consistency and alleviate rater bias. As a matter of fact, the standard procedure starts to work on rating behavior when rater training begins. PA training session regulates rating behavior in identifying and classifying propositional correspondence, developing raters' awareness of standard procedure for the assessment of information fidelity. In practice, identification and classification of propositional correspondence procedure does not leave much room for rater bias or preference, which has long been controversial in interpreting assessment. By means of SPSS and Rasch analysis, it is found that in comparison with the EIC criterion, the PA-based criterion could result in more satisfactory and consistent scoring behavior. In addition to those indicators such as rater consistency, intra-rater and inter-rater reliability, another indicator—rater bias—reveals that there is only one score with the PA-based criterion affected by rater bias. The EIC-based scores that are affected by rater bias amount to eight, with all three raters on the list. It is indicated that when working with the EIC criterion, all raters would exert their individual preference on examinees' performance, consciously or unconsciously. On the other side, PA could minimize such effect. The minimum effect of rater bias of PA is largely due to its standard assessment procedure, which consequently raises rater confidence and scoring effectiveness.

Thirdly, PA could serve as a tool in analyzing interpreting performance, especially in message transfer. For the EIC criterion, its main purpose is to assess information quality of interpreting performance. Raters, instructors or researchers would find it hard to extract other information that reveals examinees' expertise, apart from the scores themselves. PA, on the other hand, could not only score interpreting performance, but also analyze the performance of the message transfer in detail, from the perspectives of propositional correspondence features, distributions and strategy use, which could be used for analyzing general patterns, detecting prominent problems and features of certain groups of interpreters or of certain levels of interpreter trainees.

On the other hand, there are some disadvantages of PA detected during the experiment, relative to the EIC criterion. First, the PA-based criterion is labor-intensive and time-consuming. PA-based assessment runs through a procedure of text transcription, propositionalization, rater training, propositional correspondence identification and classification, which raises great demand for raters to master and command related semantic and PA-related knowledge. It also requires raters to be highly concentrative during the scoring, which is exhausting. Indicator of raters' unexpected responses from Rasch analysis reveals that drawback. Six out of seven unexpected responses of the PA-based criterion are committed by Rater C, which are considered as serious rating deviations. Post-hoc interview with Rater C shows that he was tired after long hours of scoring. Distraction for a few minutes resulted in scoring deviations. Rater C was given a second chance to reassess those segments of unexpected scores, and the subsequent scores were back in normal. This case reminds that PA raters should be warned of long-time scoring and be suggested interval rests on a regular basis.

Second, PA, focusing on propositional correspondence, tends to lead raters to omit macro-information. The logic of PA is to turn information in the source text and the interpreted text into propositions, and then match their correspondence. What raters are concentrating on is propositions, or meaning units. They may ignore information equivalence on the macro-level. Specific measures could be taken to solve the problem. First, raters should be asked to familiarize the source message in advance, so as to know the macro-structure of the source text. Further, in future assessment, raters could mark a score of macro-information fidelity to supplement a proposition-based score.

Distinctive advantages and disadvantages of the PA approach have been found during the experiment. It is possible to make full use of its advantages and keep its disadvantages at bay. Measures could be adopted to minimize or offset the disadvantages. Nevertheless, PA, as a useful assessment tool for assesssing the information fidelity of interpreting performance, could be instrumental in interpreter education, interpreting assessment and interpreting studies.

5.5 Summary

From the perspectives of theory and pracice, PA has proved to be valid in assessing information fidelity in consecutive interpreting. The theoretical part of PA has been discussed in the previous chapter. This chapter presents a comprehensive investigation into the validation procedure of the PA-based criterion on the basis of establishing Multi-Faceted Rasch Models. Following the theorization on the PA-based criterion for the assessment of information fidelity, which proves the construct validity of the criterion, quantitative results from statistical analysis are mainly presented and discussed. the PA-based criterion is measured against the EIC criterion, one currently in-use criterion for the assessment of information fidelity in interpreting test. SPSS and FACETS are the main statistical tools in present study.

The study finds out that proposition, as a standard information assessment unit, could better ensure reliable scoring results. The training procedure and stringent PA rules enable raters to achieve higher inter-rater and intra-rater reliability.

Criterion validity is validated by statistical evidence through SPSS analysis. Inter-rater reliability, and correlation analysis of the two criteria are conducted to this end. the PA-based criterion obtains higher inter-rater reliability than the EIC criterion, both in total scores and segmental scores. The findings are reinforced by Post-hoc test, which demonstrate that raters with the PA-based criterion can score examinee performance more consistently than when they are with the EIC criterion.

Evidence of rating validity is collected through MFRM. The measurement consists of three facets: examinee ability of message transfer, rater severity and segmental difficulty. Which criterion is more appropriate and feasible in the assessment of information fidelity in interpreting depends on the degree to which the criterion-based scores fit the model.

With respect to the global fit, the PA-based criterion seems to take the lead.

However, it is a double-bladed sword. While it can ensure inter-rater agreement, an overwhelming percentage of unexpected responses from a certain rater suggests that this concentration-intensive criterion needs to be taken seriously. Proper rater training is a must.

For the facet of examinee, the PA-based criterion is capable of differentiating ability of message fidelity in interpreting, and categorizing it into various levels accordingly. For the facet of rater severity, the PA-based criterion can obtain better inter-rater agreement than the EIC criterion. The conclusion is in line with that of inter-rater reliability of SPSS analysis. In addition to the data analysis of a single facet, interaction analysis between rater severity and examinee ability is conducted. It concludes that PA-based scores are less likely to be affected by rater severity or leniency, an indicator to imply that PA-based scores is a better display of examinees' ability of message transfer.

Rater training is of significance in the experiment. It is conducive to consistent rating behavior. It proves that a standardized and feasible assessment procedure, together with a fine-grained training program, could mitigate rater effects and guarantee rater reliability of the outcome.

The experiment reveals some merits and demerits of the PA-based criterion. For test designers and instructors, when considering using PA in analyzing interpreting performance, it is of importance to carry out fine-grained rater training and targeted measures, so as to check the negative effects of the demerits.

The validation procedure assures the feasibility of PA applied to the assessment of information fidelity in consecutive interpreting. However, it does not work in this area alone. In addition to scoring process, PA can tell more about students' performance, available for pedagogical use. With this, the next chapter moves on to its application and significance with respect to interpreter training. It is hoped that the involvement of PA in interpreter training will inspire trainers and trainees to tackle the thorny problems in their way and find more targeted strategies.

Chapter 6

Implications of the PA-Based Assessment for Interpreter Education

Findings in the previous chapter have offered evidence to validate the PA-based criterion in the assessment of interpreting information fidelity, and have confirmed proposition as a feasible and plausible information assessment unit emprically. In addition to its use in interpreting performance assessment, PA is also conducive to interpreting training as a source of teaching reflections and inspirations, which has rarely been touched upon. This chapter, therefore, centers around justifying that the applicability of PA is not realized in the rating process alone, but also in interpreter training. Test uses vary with test purpose, or "decision about test takers, which include selection, placement, diagnosis, progress and grading" (Bachman & Palmer, 1996:97). In other words, tests are not meant for grading alone, and they are also designed for educational purposes. After all, "much research on interpreting, has been ... more or less directly, in the service of interpreter training" (Pöchhacker, 2017:196).

To this end, this chapter explores the potential usefulness of PA for interpreter training, especially in the area of message transfer. To do so, propositions in the source Engish text and the interpreted Chinese text will be extracted and compared with reference to a classification of propostitional correspondence proposed in Chapter 4. Propositional correspondence will be further examined in view of correspondence category distribution to take a glimpse of general trends of patterning regularities of information fidelity in examinees' performance. Prominent problems existing in message transfer will surface and be examined, together with the self-perception of the examinees themselves. Lastly, PA will be applied to exploring competence trajectory of different groups of trainees, offering inspirations for interpreter instructors.

6.1 Implications from Examinees' Performance in the Message Transfer

With the categories of propositional correspondence in place, raters could assess the propositionalized texts and identify the types of propositional correspondence between the source text and the interpreted text, which results in a database of category-based propositional correspondence distribution. Propositional correspondence category data are stored in the Office Excel documents with their frequencies counted, which illustrates a rough picture of examinees' performance in message transfer. With that, the following Table 6.1 is a list of propositional pattern distribution between the source text and the interpreted text.

Table 6.1 Frequencies and Average Frequencies of Propositional
Correspondence Categories

Match			
No.	Code	Frequency	Average Frequency
1	M	9,243	70
2	M-PREED	514	4
3	M-ENTED	502	4
Match-Unclear			
No.	Code	Frequency	Average Frequency
1	M-U-PREED	317	2
2	M-U-ENTED	233	2

Continued

3	M-ALTED	2,204	6
Mismatch			
No.	Code	Frequency	Average Frequency
1	A-PSVED	293	2
2	A-ALTED	1,419	11
3	O	8,899	68
Total (Source)		21,912	166
Total (Target)		14,725	115.5

Note: Frequency is the total amount of types of propositions from three raters. Average frequency is the average amount of types of propositions per text. Total propositions are the total amount of propositions of the interpreted target texts, instead of the total amount of the listed categories of propositions, as some categories overlap.

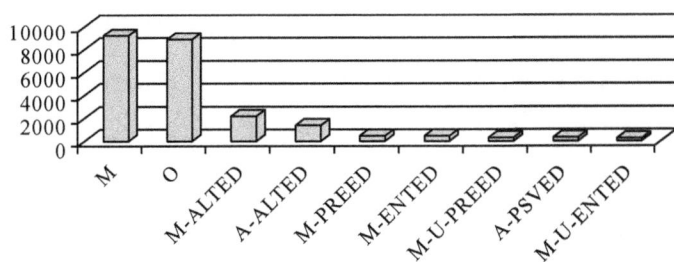

Figure 6.1 **Frequencies of Propositional Correspondence Patterns**

In general, the top 3 correspondence types are Complete Match (CM), Omission (O) and Match-Meaning Altered (M-ALTED). In the source text, there are 166 propositions, altogether there should be 21,912 propositions in the source texts for 132 sample texts (44 interpreted texts for 3 raters each). There are 14, 725 propositions in the sample texts. The largest type of propositional correspondence in scale is Match, accounting for 42.2% of the source propositions and 62.8% of the target propositions (9,243 out of 21,912 and 9,243 out of 14,725, respectively). Omission follows. There is a total amount of 8,899 propositions missing, accounting for 40.6% of the source propositions (8,899 out of 21,912). Match-Meaning altered (M-ALTED) is the biggest type in Category Match-Unclear, taking up 10.1% of the source propositions and 15.0% of the target propositions (2,204 out of 21,912 and 2,204 out of 14,725, respectively). The next sub-category of correspondence that appears more than 1,000 times is Addition-Meaning Altered (A-ALTED), which accounts for approximately 9.6% of the total target propositions. The rest correspondence types take up less than 5% of the source or target propositions. From an analytical perspective, Table 6.1 offers some clues for us to analyze examinees' interpreting performance and problems that exist in message transfer.

For starters, a comparison of the listed correspondence types reveals that two categories—Match and Mismatch (especially Omission) occupy the lion's share of propositional correspondence, which is suggestive of examinees' mental states: interpret, or keep silence. Huge differences among Complete Match (CM), Meaning Presuppose (M-PREED) and Match-Meaning Entailed (M-ENTED), as well as among Omission (O), Addition-Meaning Preserved (A-PSVED) and Addition-Meaning Altered (A-ALTED) imply that examinees incline to interpret what they are sure of, but when faced with tough issues, they are not good at handling them. On these occasions, examinees most probably give up and skip the part. The implication is backed up by examinees' responses in the questionnaire, as 31 out of 44 examinees talk about omissions in their interpreting. The following are excerpts of some responses:

1. *The biggest problem in my interpreting is that I cannot understand the whole sentence, due to insufficient vocabulary. On this occasion, I will try to omit the missing information and interpret only the information that I am sure of and try to make interpreting coherent even without the missing information.*

2. *There are some long sentences in the speech. I could not grasp*

the complete information because I cannot coordinate listening and note-taking simultaneously. I will interpret what I have noted and have to leave the missing information absent. I think no interpreting is better than misinterpreting.

3. For the information I do not know how to interpret, I will try to explain it. But when time is running out, I will circumvent and skip to the next part.

Based on examinees' responses, omissions in their message transfer mainly result from insufficient knowledge of subject matter, terminology, under-developed noting skill and active listening. More importantly, they seem to process information at lexical or phrasal levels, implying drawbacks in integrative information processing. This is in line with Hild's finding (2015), who figures out that compared to professional interpreters, who are more capable of integrative processing of semantic information, trainees allocate more cognitive resources to lexical and syntactic processing. For instructors, more efforts should be thrown into raising trainees' awareness of information processing at the macro-structure level, with more practice in summary and information outlining.

There are some attempts of employing coping tactics, as shown in Table 6.1 that Match-Meaning Entailed and Match-Meaning Presupposed rank 5th and 6th of all the nine correspondence types, which appear 514 times and 502 times respectively. Propositions of these sub-categories are considered loyal to the source propositions. (Yeh, 2015:29) The use of strategies is fairly successful, to some extent, as their counterparts (M-U-PREED and M-U-ENTED) appear 317 times and 223 times, which are considered as loyal rendition of source information. As could be seen in Excerpt 3 above, the examinee has the awareness of coping tactics to deal with tough situations, rather than merely omitting information. Instructors could make a full play of PA to summarize features of M-PREED, M-ENTED and M-U-PREED, M-U-ENTED, demonstrating trainees with the successful instances of strategy use, as well as unsuccessful ones, so as to develop their capacity of selecting appropriate strategies.

Further, Match-Meaning Altered (M-ALTED) and Addition-Meaning Altered (A-ALTED) have been detected 2,204 times and 1,419 times, ranking the third and fourth on the list respectively. These two sub-categories demonstrate twisted information, revealing faults in information processing and interpreting. The frequent appearance of M-ALTED and A-ALTED should alert the instructors that trainees have serious deficiencies in information reception and processing, which are meant to cause serious consequences. Triangulating the finding with examinees' performance, it is noticed that these twists derive from failure in "catching the idea", "coordination in multi-tasking", and "macro-level information processing". The deficiencies point to a fact that trainees are not equipped with solid bilingual knowledge, which is a major cause of problems in information reception, processing and reformulation. Instructors can deal with this problem by means of setting up courses to enhance their bilingual proficiency.

From a macro-perspective, Table 6.1 presents a picture of examinees' performance of message transfer based on PA-extracted data, which implies that examinees are not very confident, though conscious, in coping tactics, as there are too many omissions and numerous instances of strategy misuses. There are some instances of successful use of strategies, though much fewer in number. The juxtaposition of minor successful strategy use and major failed strategy use implies underdeveloped interpreting competence.

Instructors can use PA in depicting general features of trainees' performance in the message transfer, together with their outstanding problems, whereby they can detect and analyze trainees' strategy use and provide pertinent didactic suggestions in order to help them encounter the challenge in this aspect.

6.2 Implications from Correlation Between Propositional Correspondence Distribution and Performance of the Message Transfer

The previous section illustrates a rough picture of examinees' performance in terms of message transfer. Apart from that, an in-depth investigation of the database could result in more findings of examinees' interpreting performance. Correlating propositional correspondence distribution to fidelity scores would tell indicators that are key to message transfer, which is beneficial to instructors in that they could focus on the key issues in examinees' competence trajectory and facilitate competence development. Table 6.2 presents a correlation analysis of correspondence sub-categories and fidelity scores.

Table 6.2 Correlation Analysis of Correspondence Sub-Categories and Fidelity Scores

Sub-Categories		Scores
CM	Pearson Cor.	0.997[**]
	Sig.	0
M-PREED	Pearson Cor.	−0.42
	Sig.	0.789
M-ENTED	Pearson Cor.	0.128
	Sig.	0.409
M-U-PREED	Pearson Cor.	−0.205
	Sig.	−0.182
M-U-ENTED	Pearson Cor.	−0.157
	Sig.	−0.310
M-ALTED	Pearson Cor.	−0.373
	Sig.	0.013
A-ALTED	Pearson Cor.	−0.319
	Sig.	0.015

Continued

Sub-Categories		Scores
A-PSVED	Pearson Cor.	−0.082
	Sig.	0.595
O	Pearson Cor.	−0.945**
	Sig.	0

Note: "**": Correlation is significant at the 0.01 level (2-tailed)

The correlation analysis shows that two sub-categories (CM and O) are in close relationship with fidelity scores ($p = 0$, $0 < 0.01$), or examinees' performance in message transfer. CM positively correlates to fidelity scores ($r = 0.997$), which implies that the higher scores examinees get, the more CMs they achieve in interpreting. On the other hand, Omission is in negative correlation to fidelity scores, indicating that the higher score examinees get, the less instances of omission are detected in their interpreting performance.

In this sense, the two sub-categories could serve as indicators of trainees' competence in message transfer. For trainees with better interpreting competence, they are able to receive and process information properly and render it almost in the same manner as the source message. It is representative of a perfect command and use of interpreting competence.

Instructors should pay special attention to Omission, an indicator of trainees' significant problem. Omission significantly correlates to fidelity scores in a negative way ($r = -0.945$; $p = 0$), indicating that the best examinee omits the least information, vice versa. The reasons for Omission are various, extending from preparation to information reception. Based on examinees' responses, the top reasons for Omission are: insufficient preparation, vocabulary, under-developed skills of listening, noting, and information processing. It is assumed that Omission is mainly due to information loss at reception stage, signifying weakness in bilingual knowledge and interpreting skills.

The rest sub-categories do not highly correlate to fidelity scores ($p > .01$), implying that they are not predictive of interpreting competence. In addition, their frequencies in Table 6.1 are not significant relative to CM and Omission. Thus, Omission, representative of the most serious problem in trainees' performance in message transfer, deserves most attention and efforts.

For instructors, they can find solutions in dealing with this most serious problem. First and foremost, they could prioritize intensified practice and training on language proficiency. With language proficiency upgraded, trainees should have a better understanding and command of interpreting procedural knowledge, with which trainees are likely to improve their quality of interpreting performance.

6.3 Exploring Competence Trajectory of Trainees

The previous section illustrates a general picture of examinees' performance in terms of message transfer from a macro-perspective. If the database is studied with microlens, it could tell more information about examinees' performance in this regard, for instance, traits that characterize different groups of trainees could reveal different stages of interpreting competence trajectory, which explains "the path towards a type of behavior that is characteristic of consistently superior performance found among experts" (Alves, 2015: 26). Thus, it is of significance to study how interpreting competence evolves from "mere transfer of linguistically encoded items" to "the point where the translator fully integrates a more complex body of sub-competences" (ibid: 28). In interpreting studies, novice-expert paradigm is frequently adopted in this regard. For interpreting instructors, they could measure competence trajectory by comparing performance of trainees of the same or different learning stages. PA could fit well in this situation.

In the present study, examinees are all first-year trainees, so they are supposed to be at the same learning stage. However, their competence in message transfer differ greatly, as Rasch analysis reveals that their competence in this aspect is stratified into 9 levels (Separation index = 9.08). Besides competence stratification, PA can demonstrate to instructors how well-performing examinees (WE, top 25% in score) are distinguished from under-performing examinees (UE, last 25% in score), as well as their differences in competence development that underlie their performance.

The following table illustrates the frequencies and average frequencies of propositional correspondence categories of WE and UE.

Table 6.3 Frequencies and Average Frequencies of Propositional
Correspondence Categories of WE and UE

Sub-category	Total Frequency		Average Frequency (Per Person)	
	WE	UE	WE	UE
CM	4,125	1,376	125	41.7
M-PREED	95	102	2.9	3.1
M-ENTED	57	30	1.7	0.9
M-U-PREED	49	98	1.5	3
M-U-ENTED	39	44	1.2	1.3
M-ALTED	308	587	9.3	17.9
A-ALTED	131	403	4	12.2
A-PSVED	75	42	2.3	1.3
Omission	844	3,569	25.6	108
Total	4,879	2,682	147.8	81.2
Averge Score	22.3	6.1		

The table presents a list of frequencies of sub-categories of propositional analysis, from which we could draw reference for performance analysis. Complete Match (CM) accounts for 85% of all the propositions in WE's interpreted texts, while for UE's, the percentage of CM is only 51%. CM is an indicator of perfect information equivalence between the source text and the interpreted text. It means that examinees fully understand the source message and deliver them successfully, which represents examinees' capability in receiving, processing and reformulating information. The large gap between WE and UE in CM reveals that WE are far ahead in interpreting competence trajectory.

Omission ranks the second in frequency. In WE's performance, Omission has been detected 844 times, and in UE's performance, it has been detected 3,569 times. It implies that omission is in negative correlation to interpreting competence. Despite that, data analysis notifies that WE and UE are different in using omissions. That is, WE tend to use omissions when they realize information is redundant, or when omissions are actually necessary due to linguistic structural features. The following are examples:

Example 1:

Source: Globally, mobile technology has emerged as the primary engine of economic growth, generating almost \$3.3 trillion in revenue globally in 2014 and is directly responsible for 11 million jobs.

译文：(WE) 移动技术成为经济发展的动力。2014年,移动经济为全球经济创造了3.3万亿美元的收入,直接创造的工作岗位达1100万。

(UE) 全球范围内,移动经济推动了经济的发展,创造了很多的收入和数以百万计的就业岗位。

Example 2:

Source: The rapid diffusion of mobile technologies in the first decade of the new millennium has little precedent in history. No other technology has ever been in the hands of so many people in so many countries in such a short period of time.

译文：(WE) 在新世纪的头十年里,移动技术的发展是史无前例的,它迅速被众多的国家,众多的人使用。

(UE1)移动技术快速发展,在短时间内就蔓延到各个国家,人手一部。

(UE2)在过去的十年间,移动技术得到了前所未有的发展,这是之前所没有的。

In Example 1, WE omits "Globally" in interpreting, but is made up in the latter part of the sentence, because there are two "globally" in the sentence. From the perspective of PA, it does not incur information loss. Therefore, it is assessed with "Complete Match", which is analyzed below (see Table 6.4):

Table 6.4 Analysis of Example 1

No.	Source Propositions			Interpreted Propositions		
	Predicate	Argument 1	Argument 2	Predicate	Argument 1	Argument 2
1	Globally			(P5)		
2	Emerge ... as...	MB	P3	成为	移动技术	P3
3		engine	eco. growth		动力	经济发展
4	2014			2014年		
5	generating	MB	revenue	创造	移动经济	收入
6		revenue	$3.3 trillion		收入	3.3万亿美元
7	P1			全球范围内		

The case is similar in Example 2, where WE integrates information in the two sentences. When propositionalized, the integrated information will be restored, and no information loss is incurred.

Different from WE, UE tends to omit key information. In Example 1, UE omit the numerical information, which serves as Arguments in PA, leading to serious information loss. In Example 2, UE omit more information, which is rated as "Omission".

Table 6.5 Analysis of Example 2

No.	Source Propositions			Interpreted Propositions		
	Predicate	Argumtment 1	Argumtment 2	Predicate	Argumtment 1	Argumtment 2
1	first decade	new millennium		过去十年		
2	diffusion	MB	rapidly	发展	移动技术	快速
3	has	P2	precedent	有	先例	
4	NO	P3		没有		
5	USE	other technology	P6			
6	and	people	country	有	P2	先例
7	No	P5		没有		
8	in	short period of time				

Shown in the table above, P5, P6 and P8 in the source text are omitted, with P1 being an instance of mismatch. P6 in interpreted text is actually a repetition of P3. The omissions may derive from information loss in listening or note taking.

The different uses of omission by WE and UE could be explained by different causes. There are conscious strategic omissions in which interpreters "make conscious strategic decisions as an intrinsic part of the interpreting process" (Napier, 2004:123). Conscious strategic decisions are made consciously by an interpreter to omit information that is redundant or repeated, so as to enhance the effectiveness of interpreting. Other types of omissions, such as conscious intentional omissions, conscious unintentional omissions, conscious receptive omissions and unconscious omissions, are due to information loss in reception stage, or failure to recall in delivery. Napier also suggests that conscious strategic omissions from professional interpreters account for one fourth to one third of all omissions. In the present study, WE's conscious strategic omissions account for nearly 12% (97 times), while UE's conscious strategic omissions take up less than 1% (14 times). WE seem to be more aware of linguistic structural differences and use omissions more proactively to deal with information of high lexical and semantic density. One examinee writes about omission:

> I use omission when I find that the sentence is repetitive, or the information is redundant, because it could save time and ease burden for analyzing and interpreting the following information.

UE demonstrate weaker awareness of conscious strategic omissions. They omit because of failure or incompetence in any of the stages of information reception, process and reformulation. For WE, omissions may be a coping tactic, while for UE, omissions are mostly products of under-developed interpreting competence.

Instructors could use PA to distinguish conscious strategic omissions from other types of omissions. They could help trainees to get some procedural knowledge of conscious strategic omissions and find solutions to other types of omissions. As regards strategic use, Alves (2015) suggests instructors take measures to promote trainees' awareness through meta-cognitive activities, such as interpreting diary, interpreting reflection and group discussion.

In addition to WE and UE groups, PA could also facilitate analysis of competence in message transfer between groups of trainees at different levels, which is another key link of the chain of interpreting competence trajectory.

6.4 The PA-Based Assessment in Interpreter Education

6.4.1 Using PA in Instructing Information Processing

In the last section, it is discovered that information omissions constitute the most prominent problem in interpreting performance. According to the examinees' responses, there are various reasons for this problem. A fact is that all factors, such as information loss at the reception stage, under-developed skills in information processing and noting, and insufficient bilingual knowledge, contribute to this problem. As to insufficient bilingual knowledge, it could be dealt with through intensive training and deliberate practice. As to the remaining causes of the problem, instructors can deal with them by means of incorporating PA into information processing.

It has been stated that proposition, since it was introduced to psychology and cognitive science, has been regarded as a basic unit of meaning representation. It is assumed that proposition is, as a matter of fact, a piece of information represented by the lexicons at the lexico-grammatical level. Propositions serve as building blocks of discourse. In this sense, information reception is actually a process of extracting propositional information from the surface lexico-grammatical level. This theory could also explain the process of information analysis in interpreting. It is widely accepted that information process in interpreting should never focus on word-for-word analysis, but the message between the lines, a process of deverbalization. From the semantic perspective, the process of information processing is to transfer verbal elements into propositions. During the stage of reformulation, interpreters retrieve propositional information out of the short-term memory and render it into the target language, also in the form of propositional information.

This hypothesis of proposition-based interpreting can help instructors deal with the foregrounding problems in the message transfer. Information omission, the most serious problem in trainees' interpreting performance, is largely due to information loss at the stages of information reception and processing. Therefore, the key to addressing this problem lies in helping trainees improve their skill of information process, which starts with active listening. Previous research discovers that interpreter trainees are more likely to analyze information with words or phrases, units smaller than the semantic units used by professionals.

(cf. Hild, 2015) This discrepancy in units of information processing sheds light on interpreting training. It implies that professionals process information at the semantic level, and trainees process information at the lexical level, which restrains trainees' capability of processing information at a macro-level. Instructors can make use of the PA-based assessment in instructing information processing, for instance, active listening and note taking.

For starters, instructors could help trainees form a clear idea of information, which is not merely a combination of words. Trainees should be aware of the hierarchical structure of semantic information, which consists of information points, semantic structure and text base. Meanwhile, instructors could explain that proposition, basis of these constituents, also consists of some basic components of information (Predicate, Argument 1, Argument 2). In this way, trainees could develop awareness of information structure of discourse, and know about what active listening is meant for and what could be considered as key information. Furthermore, trainees could understand why key words, as well as cohesive devices, are the key to information analysis.

Instructors could remind trainees that in listening, it is possible to break down macro-information into propositions. The process of active listening is also a process of identifying propositions and propositional relations. This technique is especially useful in the discourse characterized with "high text informativity and semantic density" (Hild, 2015:94). Based on propositional analysis, trainees could learn the technique of breaking down macro-information into smaller propositions, analyzing them one at a time, which helps ease their overloaded cognitive resources and boost their efficiency in active listening.

Further, PA is useful in developing the note-taking skill. Examinees recognize that in addition to inefficiency in information processing, under-developed noting skill is also a major cause of information loss. It has been pointed out that for interpreter novices, note-taking is more like dictation, that is, trainees, without adequate information analysis, desire to note down as much as possible. As they are more skilled in interpreting, their notes are simplified and shrinking in size. (Wang & Guo, 2015) There have been discussions as to what to note. (Ji, 1996; Mu & Lei, 1998; Huang, 2005; Wang & Zhou, 2014;Wang & Guo, 2015）A consensus reached is that interpreting notes should include key information (including main structure and key words, cohesive devices), numbers, listings and proper names that are difficult to memorize. (Mu & Lei, 1998; Huang, 2005; Lei & Chen, 2006) A challenge that interpreter trainees face is that they are not capable of sorting out key information from the discourse, which they reflect in the questionnaire. PA could help them solve this problem in two aspects: first, propositions could help trainees locate key words and local coherence. PA could enable trainees to quickly break down sentences into propositional information and help them organize information with the help of cohesive devices, which facilitates information processing and storage; second, PA could help trainees note down information in a systematic and logical way. It is suggested that notes should be horizontally sequenced. (Lei & Chen, 2006) Based on PA, instructors could suggest that notes be taken one proposition at a time, one proposition in a line. Trainees would come to realize that in addition to the key words, cohesive devices, representing propositional relations, should also be noted. In a word, PA could enhance trainees' awareness of sorting out key information, which could not only facilitate information processing, but also pave the way for prompting message retrieving in time of reformulation.

Generally speaking, PA is a useful instrument for interpreter instructors, because of its potential in facilitating development of interpreting skills, such as active listening and note taking. The concept of proposition reminds trainees of what constitutes information and how to analyze information during listening. PA would develop trainees' awareness of what to note and how to note. It is of significance for instructors to introduce proposition and PA to trainees during class, which is a boost to their awareness of information processing.

6.4.2 Incorporating PA into Peer Review

For quality assessment in education contexts, there are two major types: external assessment and self assessment. (Bartłomiejczyk, 2007) External assessment is normally carried out by instructors or peers, and selfassessment is performed by trainees themselves. PA could be instrumental in both types. In this section, the author will illustrate how PA could be applied to assessment in educational contexts from the aspect of peer review.

Currently, peer review (or peer assessment) is gaining popularity in interpreter education. Peer review in interpreting refers to the assessment of interpreting performance by one or more persons with similar competences, for either summative or formative purposes. For interpreter trainees, peer review is "an authentic approach to assessing learning and achievement by fostering trainees' capabilities for critical thinking and self evaluation" (Boase-Jelinek, Parker & Herrington, 2013: 119). The benefits of peer review are many. Peer review is beneficial not only for the trainees who receive the feedback, but also for the trainees who give it. Those who experience peer review would benefit for learning by suggestions from their peers, as well as by improving their understanding of the criteria used for the assessment of their performance. Those who provide the feedback also benefit from processing and analyzing the work of a peer, and may be inspired for improving their own performance. (Sims, 1989; Wesssa & De Rycker, 2010; Wood & Kurzel, 2008)

There have been instances that instructors who had tempted to incorporate peer review into their courses reported less than satisfying results. It has been mentioned that many trainees, when asked to participate in peer review, tend to rush through the process and offer rough and general comments. One main reason for the rough comments is that trainee reviewers are not given clear guidance, unaware of how to comment in a specific and constructive way. It is proposed that a top priority in designing peer review be to develop proper peer feedback criteria for those trainee reviewers. (Boase-Jelinek, Parker & Herrington, 2013)

Interpreter instructors are facing a similar challenge. In designing peer review, it is necessary to develop clear-cut rubrics for the assessment assignment. As to the three major criteria of interpreting performance—information fidelity, delivery and target language quality, information fidelity is the most difficult to define. In this situation, instructors can turn to PA, which boasts of a standard information assessment unit and standardized assessment procedure.

Incorporating PA into peer review, instructors would find it easier to design workable feedback criteria. Rather than vague and general descriptors, PA could provide concise and clearly-defined descriptors for assessment use. Based on PA, trainee reviewers could accurately identify and assess peer performance in the message transfer and locate the problem, which leads to pertinent feedback subsequently.

Apart from smoothing reviewing process, the coding scheme of PA also facilitates feedback analysis and statistics. The standardized identification and classification procedure enables instructors to analyze trainees' peer reviewing synchronically or diachronically, keeping an eye on the development of self-monitoring and self-regulation competence. Furthermore, the standardized procedure empowers instructors to analyze how trainee reviews are similar to instructor reviews, and to what extent trainee reviews deviate from instructor reviews, both of which offer interesting pedagogical implications and inspire future studies.

To sum up, PA is useful not only in the assessment of information fidelity in consecutive interpreting, but also in pedagogy. When incorporated into interpreter education, PA can improve skillsof active listening and note taking, which is conducive to development of capability for information processing. In addition, PA could facilitate peer review for formative purposes, which is gaining popularity in interpreter education and beneficial to trainees in the long run.

6.5 Summary

This chapter, based on data extracted by means of PA, examines information correspondence distribution in the source text and the interpreted texts. More importantly, the discussion centers on how PA could be integrated in interpreter education and how it could help with analyzing interpreting performance for instruction use.

Firstly, a macro-analysis enabled by comparisons among sub-categories of propositional correspondence reveals that Complete Match, Omission and Match-Meaning Altered are the types of correspondence with most frequency, which depicts a rough picture of examinees' performance in message transfer for in-depth analysis.

Secondly, to explore in-depth pedagogical implications of those data, correlation analysis between fidelity scores and correspondence sub-categories has been conducted to shed light on critical indicators' competence in message transfer. Results show that Complete Match and Omission highly correlate to fidelity scores, positively and negatively respectively. It implies that they are predictive for competence of message rendition. As Omission is representative of the most serious problem, it is suggested that instructors should prioritize it and locate the causes of information loss at reception stage and exert intensified efforts, so as to increase the quality of trainees' interpreting performance.

Thirdly, PA is used for detecting competence trajectory of top-rated examinees and lowest-rated examinees. It is discovered that the two groups of examinees differ in the use of omissions. While the top-rated examinees tend to use omissions as conscious strategy, the lowest-rated examinees omit in a passive way, due to serious information loss. In addition to top-rated trainees and lowest-rated trainees, PA could also be used in detecting trajectory of trainees at different stages of learning.

Finally, pedagogical implications of PA are discussed from the perspectives of information processing and peer review. It mentions that PA could serve as a basic interpreting unit, which could facilitate instructions of active listening and note taking. On the other hand, PA could be incorporated into peer review, facilitating the reviewing process and reviewing analysis.

Chapter 7

Conclusions

This chapter is to present a brief summary of the present study on the PA-based information fidelity assessment in consecutive interpreting, which includes its major findings, contributions and limitations in the hope of providing some indications for further studies in this aspect.

7.1 Major Findings

By introducing propositional analysis into the assessment of information fidelity of consecutive interpreting, the present study provides a new tool for analyzing interpreting performance, for both interpreter instructors and researchers. Specifically, the PA-based criterion is validated from three aspects: construct validity, criterion validity and rater reliability. To describe construct validity of the PA-based criterion, an analytical framework is drawn upon via which information fidelity of consecutive interpreting is examined. In the study, the PA-based criterion and the EIC criterion are employed to assess information fidelity. Rating scores of both criteria are analyzed with Rasch measurement for the investigation of criterion validity and rater reliability. Subsequently, evidence of different types of correspondence is collected and sorted out in accordance with the PA-based criterion for distribution analysis. Then, further use of PA in interpreter education is discussed from the perspectives of correlation between propositional correspondence distribution and fidelity scores, competence trajectory, and incorporating PA into interpreter education.

7.1.1 QI Assessment and Propositional Analysis

A comprehensive review of theoretical and empirical research into QI assessment shows that for interpreting assessment in both professional and educational contexts, assessment criteria are still in disagreement and vary with groups of assessors, purposes and settings, especially when it comes to the assessment of information fidelity in interpreting performance. Attempts have been made with reference to linguistic theories and methodologies, but up till now have received few resonances. In addition, the links between interpreting assessment and interpreting training are historically under-studied as opposed to assessment itself and more are awaiting to be learned as to how the PA-based assessment is going to play its role in interpreter education. In connection with this, propositional analysis, deriving from semantics, is proposed to serve as a complementary instrument to the conventional methods of the assessment of information fidelity and more importantly, bridging over the gap between interpreting assessment and training with its data sufficiency and ecological validity.

7.1.2 Validation of the PA-Based Criterion

The validation procedure goes through three steps: construct validity, criterion validity and rater reliability.

The concept of proposition, as a basic unit of semantic meaning, overlaps with the notion of information fidelity. From the hierarchy of meaning realization—phonological level, lexico-grammatical level, semantic level and contextual level, the assessment of information fidelity could be achieved at semantic level, due to the use of propositional analysis. The author proposes a systemic PA-based information fidelity assessment framework in terms of propositional correspondence: Match, Match-Unclear and Mismatch. The classification realizes a match of propositional correspondence between the source text and the interpreted text at semantic level, rather than traditional indicators of lexical equivalence.

A comparison of the PA-based criterion and a conventional criterion is conducted so as to measure the efficacy of the newly-proposed criterion. Results confirm that the scores of the PA-based criterion highly correlate to those of the EIC criterion, and both criteria have achieved high inter-rater reliability, which means that they are inter-changeable. The PA-based criterion, practically, could be used for the assessment of information fidelity in consecutive interpreting.

To further validate the PA-based criterion in rating process, Multi-Faceted Rasch Measurement (MFRM) is employed. MFRM is capable of examining feasibility of the criterion from the facets of examinee ability, rater severity and criterion or segmental difficulty. It is found out that the proposed PA-based criterion performs well in the assessment of information fidelity. First, raters with the PA-based criterion are more likely to achieve inter-rater consistency than when they are working with the conventional criterion. Also, PA is less likely to cause extreme or unexpected scores. Second, the PA-based criterion can distinguish examinees' ability in the message transfer. Moreover, the PA-based criterion can minimize potential rater effects, namely, central tendency and halo effect. Third, with higher inter-rater reliability, PA can better measure examinees' ability of message transfer, free from the impact of rater bias.

The three-dimension validation procedure concludes that PA-based assessment of information fidelity in consecutive interpreting is valid and reliable, and it possesses some advantages over the conventional assessment instruments.

7.1.3 Advantages and Disadvantages of the PA-Based Criterion

During the process of validation, some distinctive advantages of PA are detected, together with some disadvantages.

Firstly, PA, adopting proposition as a basic information assessment unit, could detect and measure the message transfer in interpreting performance more accurately. Raters are more confident and accurate in information assessment, as they focus on one proposition at a time, rather than considering information equivalence at segmental level, which easily lends itself to rater expertise and perceptions of information fidelity. It is reinforced by data indicating that the PA-based criterion could achieve higher rater consistency and inter-rater and intra-rater reliability than the EIC criterion.

Secondly, PA, by offering a standardized message transfer detection and classification procedure, could facilitate raters in achieving higher consistency and alleviate rater bias. In practice, identification and classification of propositional correspondence do not leave much room for rater bias or preference. It is found out that in comparison with the EIC criterion, the PA-based criterion could result in more satisfactory and consistent scoring behavior, partially due to the standard assessment procedure and partially due to the stringent training session.

Thirdly, PA could serve as a tool in analyzing interpreting performance, especially in the message transfer. Data reveal major indicators of examinees' performance in the message transfer, which offer clues to interpreter trainers to analyze examinees' interpreting performance in this regard. In addition, PA has the potential to facilitate self and external assessment, based on its standard assessment unit and assessment procedure.

On the other hand, there have also been some disadvantages of PA detected during assessment, relative to the EIC criterion. Firstly, the PA-based criterion is labor-intensive and time-consuming. The PA-based assessment runs through a process of text transcription, propositionalization, rater training, propositional correspondence identification and classification, which raises great demand for raters to master and command related semantic and PA-related knowledge. It also requires raters to be highly concentrative during the scoring, which is exhaustive.

Secondly, PA, focusing on propositional correspondence, tends to lead raters to turn a blind eye to macro-information. What raters are concentrating on is proposition, or meaning unit. They may ignore information equivalence on a macro-level.

Despite the disadvantages, it is possible to make full use of its advantages and keep its disadvantages at bay. For example, raters could be asked to take interval breaks, so as to refresh and ease themselves of exhaustion. Further, raters could be asked to assess macro-information fidelity, in addition to micro-information fidelity. It is no doubt that with proper measures taken, test designers or trainers could mitigate negative effects to a large extent. After all, advantages of the PA-based criterion outweigh its disadvantages.

7.1.4 Implications of PA for Interpreter Education

The inquiry of the PA-based criterion has also identified some features regarding the general distribution of propositional correspondence in the database, which also offers implications for interpreter education. Specifically, a macro-analysis of the three categories of propositional correspondence shows that Complete Match, Omission and Match-Meaning Altered are the top three most frequent types of correspondence. The rest types show signs of successful and full use of interpreting strategies.

In a much closer analysis, a microcosmic probe into the correspondence types demonstrates high correlation between fidelity scores and these sub-categories. Of all these types, only Complete Match and Omission correlate to fidelity scores, showing that these two types could serve as indicators to predict fidelity scores. Omission is representative of the most serious deficiency in examinees' performance, which points to a weak bilingual knowledge and under-developed interpreting skills. With the most serious problem pinpointed, instructors can throw concentrative efforts to enhance examinees' language proficiency in the first place.

The findings of the investigation also apply to the exploration of competence trajectory of different kinds of trainees. It is noted that upper-end examinees (WE) and lower-end examinees (UE) vary in the use of omission. Top examinees use omission as a conscious strategy, which signifies advanced competence of information processing. On the other side, lower-end examinees omit in a passive way, mainly due to serious drawbacks at information reception, processing or reformulation stages. It is necessary for instructors to distinguish conscious strategic omissions from passive omissions, and to find solutions to increase meta-cognition of trainees, so as to increase their quality of interpreting performance.

This study also offers implications for interpreting pedagogy. Instructors can make use of PA to instruct trainees how to conduct proposition-based information processing. PA could facilitate skill development, such as active listening and note taking. In addition, instructors can incorporate PA into peer review in formative assessment, whose standard procedure could facilitate reviewing process and analysis.

7.2 Contributions of the Study

The present study is based upon theories and methodologies from research on interpreting studies, linguistics and testing theories, which may reciprocate the fields in one way or another.

First, in an attempt to explore objectivity and accuracy of interpreting assessment, this study adopts PA to investigate its validity and efficacy in the assessment of information fidelity, which has attracted scholars' attention recently. It thus enriches the scope and practice of interpreting assessment and interpreting studies as a whole, wherein PA, as an assessment tool, can play a significant role.

Second, MFRM has aroused great interest among applied linguists and test designers and yielded abundant insights into the intertwined rating results in the past decade. However, its strengths in analyzing rating-related issues are yet to be further explored and exploited in the field of interpreting assessment. As rating results of interpreting performance are prone to controversy and criticism, MFRM offers a solid theoretical framework and concrete data to ensure reliability of test results and research findings. With that said, this study is a worthy attempt to explore the applicability of MFRM in interpreting assessment and subsequent data analysis.

Third, the study offers a framework of the PA-based criterion for the assessment of information fidelity. The criterion, drawing reference from semantics, can better free raters from subjectivity to ensure that rating results are better reflections of examinees' interpreting competence, free from unwanted rater bias. Further, the PA-based criterion validation procedure could serve as a reference for future studies.

Fourth, the study will facilitate links between interpreting assessment and interpreter education. It is widely acknowledged that assessment and training are inter-related, and it is equally acknowledged that many instructors are unaware of what and how to explore the test use in training. This dissertation could inspire instructors to make use of assessment-elicited data in service of interpreter education. In particular, the current investigation explores into the possible use of assessment results in interpreting pedagogy.

Last but not least, the study will benefit the budding machine-based interpreting assessment research, which is now in need of a set of machine-readable scales and criteria. The standard procedure of PA is suitable for machine-readable programs, which will greatly boost the realization and implementation of the machine-based interpreting assessment.

7.3 Limitations and Future Directions

The study has proposed and validated the PA-based criterion in the assessment of information fidelity in consecutive interpreting and subsequently explored its application in didactic aspects, which offers theoretical, practical and methodological insights into interpreting assessment. However, it is admitted that findings of this study are subject to some deficiencies and further research is in requirement in these aspects.

One of the general limitations of the study is that the data extracted are not conclusive, as the study only covers single dimension directionality (English to Chinese) and one interpreting mode (consecutive interpreting). It is unclear whether a variation of interpreting directionality or interpreting mode would result in different findings. For instance, in simultaneous interpreting, interpreters are likely to adopt different strategies from those in consecutive interpreting. And PA may need some adaptations accordingly. Thus, further expansion of the scope of PA is necessary if more variables like directionality and interpreting mode are taken in. The application of PA to the assessment of sign language interpreting should also be paid due respect. It is intriguing and meaningful to investigate the feasibility of PA in sign language interpreting and see to the necessary adaptations in practice.

Another limitation pertains to a perennial deficiency of propositional analysis, which is that PA is time- and manpower-consuming. For large-scale interpreting tests, PA is too complicated and time-consuming to be practical and affordable, which is why PA is limited in use in practice. With respect to this issue, further research on the PA-based machine assessment is necessary.

Further, the study adopts a mixture of quantitative and qualitative research methods. Quantitative research methods are employed to conduct statistical analysis, triangulated with data from the questionnaire for examinees. However, raters are not surveyed in terms of rater confidence of the PA-based criterion, which offers fresh insights for the validity and feasibility of the criterion, apart from IRRs. It deserves our attention to explore new evidence of the criterion from the rater perspective.

Lastly, talking of pedagogical implications, the author only concerns the potential use of PA in interpreting pedagogy, leaving behind empirical investigations to check the pedagogical usefulness. As this is an indispensable part of verifying practicality of PA, it leaves an intriguing issue for future study.

With respect to examinees' performance, instances of upper-end examinees and lower-end examinees are compared to illustrate their difference in strategy use. It is a pity that, due to the time limit, professionals are not included in this study, an ideal subject group to study strategy use in the expert-novice paradigm. In addition to the synchronic study exemplified in present study, future diachronic studies of how trainees develop their interpreting strategy awareness, or meta-cognition awareness would shed light on learners' competence trajectory, which, for sure, deserves our attention and efforts.

Appendix

E-C Passage for Consecutive
Interpreting Test

Directions: Please listen to the description of the situation first, and then interpret each segment at each pause.

Situation: *An analyst from an American research institute speaks to a group of leaders from small and medium-sized enterprises (SMEs) about mobile technologies and their impact on the economy, their industry and SMEs.*

Ladies and gentlemen,

Good morning. It's a privilege for me to speak about mobile technologies. By mobile, I refer to all technologies that enable voice and data services via cellular connectivity, including second generation (2G), third generation (3G), and fourth generation (4G) networks. (2 分) The rapid diffusion of mobile technologies in the first decade of the new millennium has little precedent in history. No other technology has ever been in the hands of so many people in so many countries in such a short period of time. Mobile technologies have transformed the way we live, work, play, learn, travel, and shop. Nearly all fundamental human activities have been touched, if not revolutionized, by mobile. (3 分)// (*S1 : 5 分*)

Globally, mobile technology has emerged as the primary engine of economic growth, generating almost $3.3 trillion in revenue globally in 2014 and is directly responsible for 11 million jobs. But mobile is not just an industry in and of itself. It is also the foundation upon which an impressive array of industries—new and old—have taken root and flourished. (2分)

In emerging markets, China has led the way in embracing this technology. In 2012, China became the world's largest smartphone market. Mobile represents 3.7 percent of China's GDP, with a 17.7 percent compound annual growth rate from 2009 to 2014. China is now home to more innovators in mobile technology than any other country other than the U.S. and Republic of Korea. (2分)// (*S2:4分*)

Mobile has been a driving force in the success of some of the world's most valuable companies: 6 of the top 25 most valuable companies in the world are participants in the mobile value chain, including companies such as Apple, Google, China Mobile, Alibaba and Facebook. Facebook alone grew 78 percent year-over-year between 2009 and 2013, with mobile currently representing 88 percent of its user base and accounting for approximately 66 percent of its revenue. All the major players in the mobile economy have benefited tremendously from advances in the core technologies that enable mobile communications. (4分)

Mobile is also driving intense innovation in the start-up community as well: 37 billion U.S. dollars, or 7.9 percent of all venture capital funding in 2014 was invested in mobile start-ups, up from 3.8 percent in 2010. (1分)// (*S3:5分*)

Now I would like to focus on the relationship between SME's adoption of mobile technology and their performance. We surveyed approximately 3,500 SME decision-makers in the U.S., Germany, Republic of Korea, Brazil, China, and India—six of the world's largest and most diverse economies—and took an inventory of their companies' mobile adoption levels. (2分)

In both developed and emerging markets, we found that mobile has been widely adopted by SMEs. Of the small businesses we surveyed, 90 percent report that their top managers use mobile devices regularly. And 50 to 70 percent of these companies pay for the cost of mobile devices and/or service costs for their employees. But while SMEs report a high level of penetration, they vary widely in their level of engagement. Whether in emerging or developed markets, SMEs that have embraced advanced, data-driven mobile capabilities have fared better than their peers. (3分)// (*S4:5分*)

SMEs that are mobile leaders are winning. For them, mobile has proven to be an enormous blessing. Typically, the 25 percent of SMEs that use mobile services more intensively see their revenues grow up to two times faster and add jobs up to eight times faster than their peers. (2分)

At the other end of the spectrum are the mobile laggards. Mobile laggards generally have low levels of technology adoption and limited mobile presence. Laggard SMEs have not yet integrated well-established tools into their business models, much less explored the benefits of more sophisticated technologies. They have revenue growth and job creation that substantially trail behind the leaders. With few plans to invest in mobile, these SMEs are at risk of being left behind even further. (3分) // (*S5:5分*)

The "mobile divide" between leaders and laggards—that is, the difference in growth associated with a disparity in mobile adoption—is poised to increase going forward. In the six countries that we have evaluated, closing the mobile divide among SMEs could add 7 million jobs over the next three years. It could also increase GDP growth by 0.5 percentage points and help reduce unemployment by more than 10 percent. In countries like Germany or the U.S., where high unemployment has been a problem over the past five years, closing the mobile divide could help reduce unemployment by as much as 15 to 30 percent. // (*S6:3分*)

Ladies and gentlemen,

Despite the enormous investments that have already been made in mobile technologies, we are still at the dawn of mobile's history. For this industry to sustain its extraordinary impact on jobs, economic growth, and technological progress, enormous levels of innovation are still needed. This innovation will drive the next generation of devices, create new growth opportunities for mobile players across the value chain, and ensure that the promise of the mobile revolution is fully realized for SMEs and consumers. // *(S7:3分)*

****** （**End of the Test**）

EIC Rating Scale and Assessment Sheet (Information Quality)

Table 1   EIC Rating Scale

内容	描述	等级
信息忠实度	完整传达演讲者的信息(例如：>90%)，信息基本无误，基本无漏译和错译	5
	除了个别次要信息有遗漏外，演讲者的全部重要信息都得到传达(例如：>80%)。漏译和错译较少	4
	准确度一般，但基本能够传达演讲者的信息(例如：60%—70%)，有少量漏译，但无严重错译	3
	信息传达不准确(例如：40%—50%)，存在数个重大漏译或错译现象	2
	词不达意，曲解或歪曲原文信息(例如：<30%)。漏译和错译非常严重	1

(评分员请根据细则和等级对口译录音进行评估，并按照段落赋分相应给分。)

Table 2   Assessment Sheet

考生编号			
英译汉信息传递(30分)得分：			
S1(5分)		S5(5分)	
S2(4分)		S6(3分)	
S3(5分)		S7(3分)	
S4(5分)			

Questionnaire for Interpreter Trainees

亲爱的同学：

您好！我目前正在开展一项关于口译测试与教学的研究，恳请得到您的帮助。

本人承诺，此次调查得到的所有数据仅供本人科学研究使用，绝不用于商业用途。本人保证绝不泄露您的个人信息。如需核实本人信息或了解本人研究进展，请与我联系（手机：1775059××××；邮箱：xr0×××@qq.com）。

衷心感谢您的理解和支持！

性别：_____   年龄：_____

口译学习时长：_____年   是否翻译本科毕业：_____（是/否）

口译资格证书：_____（有/无）

如有，请选择：_____

A. CATTI口译资格证书（二级/三级）

B. 上海口译资格证书（高级/中级）

C. 厦门大学口译资格证书（一级/二级/三级）

口译实践：_____小时

1. 接到口译任务后,您一般怎么准备?

2. 就此次口译测试而言,您认为您的译前准备工作怎么样? 在哪些方面可以改进?

3. 在口译过程中,您认为口译的主要问题在哪些方面? 主因是什么?

4. 就此次口译测试而言,您认为口译学习在哪些方面还需要改进?(如学习方法、学习策略、知识结构等)

5. 就此次口译测试而言,您认为教师从哪些方面可以帮助您改进?(如译前准备、练习材料、口译技巧、百科知识、实践等)

References

ALTMAN J, 1990. What helps effective communication? Some interpreters' view [J]. The interpreters' newsletter, 3(1): 23-32.

ALTMAN J, 1994. Error analysis in the teaching of simultaneous interpretion: a pilot study[G]//LAMBERT S, MOSER-MERCER B. Bridging the gap: empirical research in simultaneous interpretation. Amsterdam: John Benjamins: 25-38.

ANON, 2010. Presuppositions[M]//MALMKJÆR K. The Routledge linguistic encyclopedia. 3rd ed. London: Routledge: 419-420.

BAILEY K, 1996. Working for wash back: a review of the wash back concept in language testing[J]. Language testing, 13(3):253-279.

BARIK H C, 1971. A description of various types of omissions, additions and errors of translation encountered in simultaneous interpretation[J]. Meta, 16(4): 199-210.

BARIK H C, 1975. Simultaneous interpretation: qualitative and linguistic data[J]. Language and speech, 18(3): 272-297.

BEALER G, 1998. Propositions[J]. Mind, 107: 1-32.

BERK-SELIGSON S, 1988. The impact of politeness in witness testimony: the influence of the court interpreter[J]. Multilingua, 7(4): 411-439.

BERK-SELIGSON S, 1989. The role of register in the bilingual courtroom: evaluative reactions to interpreted testimony[J]. International journal of the sociology of language, 79(1):79-91

BOASE-JELINEK D, PARKER J, HERRINGTON J, 2013. Student reflection and learning through peer reviews[J]. Issues in educational research, 23(2): 119-131.

BOVAIR S, KIERAS D, 1981. A guide to propositional analysis for research on technical prose[J]. Computer Science. DOI: 10.432411978131509995812..

BÜHLER H, 1986. Linguistic (semantic) and extra-linguistic (pragmatic) criteria for the evaluation of conference interpretation and interpreters[J]. Multilingua, 5(4): 231-235.

CARROLL J B, 1978. Linguistic abilities in translators and interpreters[G]// GERVER D, SINAIKO H W. Language interpretation and communication. New York: Plenum Press: 119-129.

CHIARO D, NOCELLA G, 2004. Interpreters' perception of linguistic and non-linguistic factors affecting quality: a survey through the world wide web[J]. Meta, 49(2): 278-293.

COLLADOS AÍS Á, 2002. Quality assessment in simultaneous interpreting: the importance of nonverbal communication[G]//Pöchhacker F, Shlesinger M. The Interpreting Studies Reader. London and New York: Routledge: 326-336.

COOK D A, et al., 2008. Effect of rater training on reliability and accuracy of mini-cex scores: a randomized, controlled trial[J]. Journal of General Internal Medicine, 24(1): 74-79.

CRAWFORD S, 2006. Propositions[M]//Brown K, et al. Encyclopedia of language and linguistics. 2nd ed. Amsterdam: Elsvier: 8631-8635.

CRONBACH L J, MEEHL P E, 1955. Construct validity in psychological tests [J]. Psychological bulletin, 52(3): 281-301.

DANIEL G, 1999. Testing the Effort Models ' tightrope hypothesis in simultaneous interpreting—a contribution[J]. Hermes, 23:153-172.

DANIEL G, 2011. Errors, omissions and infelicities in broadcast interpreting: Preliminary findings from a case study[G]//ALVSTAD C, HILD A, TISELIUS

E. Methods and Strategies of Process Research: Integrative Approaches in Translation Studies. Amsterdam: John Benjamins: 201-218.

DEJEAN LE FÉAL K, 1998. Some thoughts on the evaluation of simultaneous interpretation[G]//Bowen D. Interpreting yesterday, today, and tomorrow. Amsterdam: John Benjamins: 154-160.

Dillinger M L, 1989. Component processes of simultaneous interpreting[M]. McGill University.

Dillinger M L, 1994. Comprehension during interpreting: what do interpreters know that bilinguals don't? [G]//LAMBERT S, MOSER-MERCER B. Bridging the gap: empirical research in simultaneous interpretation. Amsterdam: John Benjamins: 155-190.

ECKES T, 2015. Introduction to many-facet rasch measurement[M]. 2nd ed. Frankfurt: Peter Lang.

ERICSSON A, 2001. Expertise in interpreting: an expert-performance perspective [J]. Interpreting, 5(2):187-220.

ERICSSON A, CHARNESS N, 1997. Cognitive and developmental factors in expert performance[G]//FELTOVICH P J, et al. Expertise in Context: Human and Machine. Cambridge: MIT Press.

ERICSSON A, CHARNESS N, FELTOVICH P J, et al., 2006. The Cambridge Handbook of Expertise and Expert Performance[M]. Cambridge: Cambridge University Press.

FRASER B, FREEDGOOD L, 1999. Interpreter alterations to pragmatic features in trial testimony[C]//Paper presented at the annual meeting of the American Association for Applied Linguistics 21. Stanford, CA: American Association for Applied Linguistics.

GALE R M, 1967. Proposition, judgments, sentences and statements[M]// EDWARDS P. The Encyclopedia of philosophy: vol. 6. New York, Macmillan: 494-505.

GILE D, 1991. A communication-oriented analysis of quality in nonliterary translation and interpretation[G]//LARSON M L. Translation: theory and practice. tension and interdependence. Binghamton, NY: SUNY, 5: 188-200.

GILE D, 1995. Fidelity Assessment in Consecutive Interpretation: An Experiment [J]. Target, 7(1): 151-164.

GILE D, 2003. Quality assessment in conference interpreting: methodological issues [M]//COLLADOSAÍS M, FERNÁNDEZ S, GILE D. La Evaluación de la Calidad en Interpretación. Granada Comares: 109-123.

GILE D, 2009. Basic Concepts and Models for Interpreter and Translator Training[M]. Amsterdam: John Benjamins.

GILED, 2011. Errors, omissions and infelicities in broadcast interpreting. [G]// ALVSTAD C, HILD A, TISELIUS E. Methods and Strategies of Process Research. Amsterdam: John Benjamins: 201-218.

GONSALEZ R D, VASQUEZ V E, MIKKELSON H, 1991. Fundamentals of court interpreting: theory, policy, and practice[M]. Durham, N. C.: Carolina Academic Press.

GRBIĆ N, 2008. Constructing interpreting quality[J]. Interpreting, 10(2): 232-257.

HALE S, 1997. The Treatment of Register Variation in Court Interpreting[J]. The translator, 31: 39-54.

HALE S, 2007. Community Interpreting[M]. New York: Palgrave Macmillan.

HAMERS J F, LEMIEUX S, LAMBERT S, 2002. Does early bilingual acquisition affect hemispheric preferences during simultaneous interpretation?[J]. Meta, 47 (3): 586-595.

HAN C, 2015. Investigating rater severity/leniency in interpreter performance testing—a Multi-Faceted Rasche Measurement approach[J]. Interpreting, 17 (2): 255-283.

HAN C, 2016. Reporting practices of rater reliability in interpreting research: a mixed-methods review of 14 journals (2004—2014) [J]. Journal of research design and statistical in linguistics and communication science, 3(1): 49-75.

HAN C, 2018. Using rating scales to assess interpretation—practices, problems and prospects[J]. Interpreting, 20(1): 60-96.

HAN C, SLAYTER H, 2016. Test validation in interpreter certification performance testing: an argument-based approach[J]. Interpreting, 18(2):231-258.

HEARN J, CHESHER T, HOLMES S, 1981. An evaluation of interpreter programmes in relation to the needs of a polyethnic society and the implications for education [EB/OL responses](2017-10-02)[2018-18-12].http://www. certifedmedicalinterpreters. org/sites/default/fles/tech-report-development-validationlanguage-forms.pdf

HOUSE J, 1997. Translation quality assessment: a model revisited[M]. Tübingen: Gunter Narr Verlag.

HOUSE J, 2014. Translation quality assessment: past and present[M]. London and New York: Routledge.

ISHAM W P, LANE H, 1993. Simultaneous interpretation and the recall of source-language sentences[J]. Language and cognitive processes, 8(3): 241-264.

JAMES C, 2001. Errors in language learning and use: exploring error analysis [M]. Beijing: Foreign Language Teaching and Research Press.

JUBINE M, 2001. Propositions and the objects of thought[J]. Philosophical studies, 104(1): 47-62.

KAHANE E, 2000. Thoughts on the quality of interpretation[EB/OL].(2018-04-01)[2021-11-12]. https://aiic.net/p/197.

KALINA S, 1994. Analyzing interpreters' performance: methods and problems [G]//DOLLERUP C, LODDEGAARD, A. Teaching translation and interpreting 2: insights, aims, visions. Amsterdam: John Benjamins: 225-232.

KEARNS K, 2011. Semantics[M]. 2nd ed. Hampshire and New York: Palgrave.

KINCAID J P, FISHBURNE R P, ROGERS R L, et al., 1975. Derivation of new readability formulas (automated readability index, fog count, and flesch reading ease formula) for Navy enlisted personnel[R]. Chief of Naval Technical Training: Naval Air Station Memphis: 8-75.

KINTSCH W, 2014. The representation of meaning in memory[M]. New York,

Toronto, London and Sydney: John Wiley & Sons.

KINTSCH W, VAN DIJK T A, 1978. Toward a model of text comprehension and production[J]. Psychological review, 85(5): 363-394.

KNOCH U, CHAPELLE C A, 2017. Validation of rating processes within an argument-based framework[J]. Language testing. DOI: 10.1177/0265532217710049.

KOPCZYŃSKI ANDRZEJ, 1994. Quality in Conference Interpreting : some pragmatic problems[G]//SNELL-HORNBY M, PÖCHHACKER F, KAINDL K. Translation Studies: An Interdiscipline. Amsterdam: John Benjamins. 189-198.

KROUGLOV A, 1999. Police interpreting[J]. The translator, 5(2): 285-302.

KUO D, FAGAN M, 1999. Satisfaction with methods of Spanish interpretation in an ambulatory care clinic[J]. Journal of general and internal medicine, 14(9): 547-550.

KURZ I, 2001. Conference interpreting: quality in the ears of the user [J]. Meta, 46(2): 394-409.

KURZ I, 2002. Conference interpretation: expectations of different user groups [G]// PÖCHHACKER F, SHLESINGER M. The interpreting studies reader. London and New York: Routledge: 312-324.

LEE J, 2008. Rating scales for interpreting performance assessment[J]. The interpreter and translator trainer, 2(2): 165-184.

LEE S-B, 2015. Developing an analytical scale for assessing undergraduate students' consecutive interpreting performances[J]. Interpreting, 17(2): 226-254.

LEE T S, LANSBURY G, SULLIVAN G, 2005. Health care interpreters: a physiotherapy perspective[J]. Australian journal of physiotherapy, 5(1):161-165.

LEE TAE-HYUNG, 1999. Speech proportion and accuracy in simultaneous interpretation from English into Korean [J]. Meta, 44(2):260-267.

LEECH G N, 1974. Semantics[M]. Harmondsworth: Peguin Books.

LEMIEUX S, HAMERS J, 1995. Hemispheric involvement and information processing in simultaneous interpretation[J]. Brain and cognition, 30(3):

354-357.

LINACRE J M, 2005. A User's Guide to FACETS[M]. Chicago: MESA Press.

LÖRSCHER W, 1991. Translation performance, translation process, and translation strategies: a psycholinguistic investigation[M]. Tubingen: G, Narr.

LÖRSCHER W, 2005. The translation process: methods and problems of its investigation[J]. Meta, 50(2): 597-608.

MACK G, CATTARUZZA L, 1995. User surveys in SI: a means of learning about quality and/or raising some reasonable doubts[C]//TOMMOLA J. Topics in interpreting research. Turku: Centre for Translation and Interpreting, University of Turku: 37-49.

MACKINTOSH J, 1983. Relay Interpretation: An Exploratory Study[M]. London: University of London.

MACKINTOSH J, 1985. The Kintsch and Van Dijk model of discourse comprehension and production applied to the interpretation process[J]. Meta, 30(1): 37-43

MARRONE S, 1993. Quality: a shared objective[J]. The Interpreters' Newsletter, 5: 35-41.

MCNAMARA T, 1996. Measuring Second Language Performance[M]. Harlow: Addison Wesley Longman.

MEAD P, 2005 Methodological issues in the study of interpreters' fluency [J]. The interpreters' newsletter, 1(3): 39-63.

MOSER-MERCER B, 1996. Quality in interpreting: some methodological issues [J]. The interpreters' newsletter, 7: 43-55.

MYFORD C M, WOLFE E W, 2000. Monitoring sources of variability within the Test of Spoken English assessment system (TOEFL Research Report No. 65)[R]. Princeton, NJ: Educational Testing Service.

NG B C, 2000. End-users' subjective reaction to the performance of student interpreters [J]. The interpreters' newsletter (special issue): 35-41.

PADILLA P, BAJO M T, PADILLA F, 1999. Proposal for a cognitive theory of translation and interpreting[J]. The interpreters' newsletter, 9: 61-78.

PERRIG W, KINTSCH W, 1985. Propositional and situational representations of text[J]. Journal of memory and language, 2(4): 503-518.

PÖCHHACKER F, 1994. Quality assurance in simultaneous interpreting[G]// DOLLERUP C, LINDEGAARD A. Teaching Translation and Interpreting 2: Insights, Aims, Visions. Amsterdam: John Benjamins: 232-242.

PÖCHHACKER F, 2001. Quality assessment in conference and community interpreting[J]. Meta, 46(2): 410-425.

PÖCHHACKER F, 2011. Assessing aptitude for interpreting[J]. Interpreting, 13 (1):106-120.

PÖCHHACKER F, GRBIĆ N, MEAD P, 2015. Routledge encyclopedia of interpreting studies[M]. London: Routledge.

PÖCHHACKER F, SHLESINGER M, 2000. The interpreting studies reader[M]. London and New York: Routledge.

PULAKOS E D, 1984. A comparison of rater training programs: error training and accuracy training[J]. Journal of applied psychology, 69(3): 581-588.

RICCARDI A, 2002. Evaluation in interpretation: Macro-criterion and micro-criterion[G]//HUNG E. Teaching translation and interpreting 4: building bridges. Amsterdam: John Benjamins: 115-126.

RICHARDS J, PLATT J, 2002. Longman Dictionary of Language Teaching and Applied Linguistics[M]. Beijing: Foreign Language Teaching and Research Press.

RINNE J O, TOMMOLA J, LAINE M, et al., 2000. The translating brain: cerebral activation patterns during simultaneous interpreting[J]. Neuroscience letters, 294(2): 85-88.

ROAT C E, 2006. Certification of health care interpreters in the United States: a primer, a status report and considerations for national certification[M]. [2017-10-02]. http://www. calendow. org/uploadedFiles/certifcation_of_health_care_interpretors. pdf.

ROSIERS A, EYCKMANS J, BAUWENS D, 2011. A story of attitudes and aptitudes? Investigating individual difference variables within the context of interpreting[J]. Interpreting, 13(1): 53-69.

RUSSO M, 2011. Aptitude testing over the years[J]. Interpreting, 13(1): 5-30.

RYLE G, 2002. The concept of mind[M]. Chicago: University of Chicago Press.

SAIF S, 1999. Theoretical and empirical considerations in investigating wash back: a study of ESL/EFL learners[D]. Toronto: University of Victoria.

SHAW S, 2011. Cognitive and motivational contributions to aptitude: a study of spoken and signed language interpreting students[J]. Interpreting, 13(1): 70-84.

SHLESINGER M, PÖCHHACKER F, 2011. Aptitude for interpreting[J]. Interpreting, 13(1): 1-4.

SHLESINGER, M. 1994. Intonation in the production and perception of simultaneous interpretation[G]//LAMBERT S, MOSER-MERCER B. Bridging the gap: empirical research in simultaneous interpretation. Amsterdam: John Benjamins: 225-236.

SIMS G K, 1989. Student peer review in the classroom: a teaching and grading tool[J]. Journal of agronomic education, 18(2): 105-108.

SMITH M K, 2000. Curriculum theory and practice[M]. [2018-08-09]. http://www.infed.org/biblio/b-curric.htm.

STRAWSON P F, 1950. On referring[J]. Mind, 5(9): 320-344.

SUNNARI M, 1995. Processing strategies in simultaneous interpreting: "saying-it-all" vs. synthetic[G]//TOMMOLA J. Topics in interpreting research. Turku, Finland: University of Turku, Centre for Translation and Interpreting: 109-119.

TEBBLE H, 1999. The Tenor of Consultant Physicians[J]. The translator, 5(2): 179-200.

THOMAS J, 1983. Cross-cultural pragmatic failure[J]. Applied linguistics, 4(2): 91-111.

THOMAS J, HELEVÄ M, 1998. Language direction and source text complexity: effects on trainee performance in simultaneous interpreting[C]//Bowker L,

Cronin M, Kenny D, et al. Unity in diversity? Current trends in translation studies[C]. Manchester: St. Jerome Publishing: 177-186.

THOMAS J, LINDHOLM J, 1995. Experimental research on interpreting: which dependent variable?[G]//TOMMOLA J. Topics in interpreting research. Turku, Finland: University of Turku: 121-133.

TOMMOLA J, LAINE M, SUNNARI M, et al., 2000. Images of shadowing and interpreting[J]. Interpreting, 5(2), 147-169.

TURNER A, GREENE E, 1977. The Construction and use of a propositional text base[M]. Boulder, CO: University of Colorado, Lnstitute for the Study of Intellectual Behavior.

VANDEPITTER V, HARTSUIKER R J, VAN ASSCHE E, 2015. Process and text studies of a translation problem[G]//FERREIRA A, SCHWIETER J W. Psycholinguistic and cognitive inquiries into translation and interpreting. Amsterdam: John Benjamins, 127-143.

VASQUEZ C, JAVIER R A, 1991. The problem with interpreters: communicating with Spanish-speaking patients[J]. Hospital and community psychiatry, 42(2): 163-165.

VUORIKOSKI A, 1998. User responses to simultaneous interpreting[G]// BOWKER L, PEARSON J. Unity in Diversity? Current Trends in Translation Studies. Manchester: St. Jerome Publishing: 187-196.

WEIR C J, 2005. Language testing and validation: an evidence-based approach [M]. New York: Palgrave Macmillan.

WESSA P, DE RYCKER A, 2010. Reviewing peer reviews: a rule-based approach[C]// ICEL. Proceedings of 5th International Conference on e-Learning. Penang: ICEL: 408-418.

WILSS W, 1978. Syntactic anticipation in German-English simultaneous interpreting[G]//GERVER D, SINAIKO H W. Language interpretation and communication. New York: Plenum Press: 343-352.

WOOD D, KURZEL F, 2008. Engaging students in reflective practice through a process of formative peer review and peer assessment[C]//JOHSTON H, AZIZ S M, KAYA C Y, ATN Assessment Conference 2008: engaging students in assessment. [2018-10-24]. http://www. ojs. unisa. edu. au/index. php/atna/article/download/376/252.

XIAO R, YU H, 2017. Review of global trends in translator and interpreter training: mediation and culture[J]. The interpreter and translator trainer, 11(1): 98-102.

鲍刚,2011. 口译理论概述[M]. 北京:中国对外翻译出版公司.

蔡小红,2001. 交替传译过程及能力发展:中国法语译员和学生的交替传译活动实证研究[J]. 现代外语,24(3):276-284.

蔡小红,2001. 以跨学科的视野拓展口译研究[J]. 中国翻译,22(2):26-29.

蔡小红,2003. 论口译质量评估的信息单位[J]. 外国语(5):75-80.

蔡小红,2007. 口译评估[M]. 北京:中国对外翻译出版公司.

陈菁,2002. 从 Bachman 交际法语言测试理论模式看口译测试中的重要因素[J]. 中国翻译(1):51-53.

陈菁,2003. 交际法原则指导下的口译测试的具体操作[J]. 中国翻译(1):67-71.

范志嘉,2006. 口译质量评估中的用户期望[D]. 成都:四川大学.

封裕,2015. 英汉双语交替传译中隐喻的理解与表达:一项基于口译专业研究生的实验报告[D]. 呼和浩特:内蒙古大学.

冯建中,2005. 论口译测试的规范化[J]. 外语研究(1):54-58.

高宁,2017. 逻辑素与翻译单位研究[J]. 外语教学理论与实践(3):72-79.

郭建中,2001. 汉译英的翻译单位问题[J]. 外国语(6):49-56.

郭修敏,2016. 汉语口语成绩测试评分员培训体系建构及实证研究[J]. 语言教学与研究,1:24-31.

何慧玲,2002. 从功能性的观点探讨国际会议中英口译之评估[G]// 蔡小红. 口译研究新探:新方法、新观点、新倾向. 香港:开益出版社:349-362.

胡开宝,陶庆,2009. 汉英会议口译中语篇意义显化及其动因研究:一项基于平行语料库的研究[J]. 解放军外国语学院学报(3):67-73.

雷天放,陈菁,2006. 口译教程[M]. 上海:上海外语教育出版社.

李文中,2010.平行语料库设计及对应单位识别[J].当代外语研究(9):22-27.

李英,2014.PETS口试评分培训效果研究[J].中国外语,59(3):69-77.

李英,关丹丹,2016.PETS口试评分培训效果的多面Rasch分析[J].外语教学理论与实践(3):43-48.

刘和平,2005.口译理论与教学[M].北京:中国对外翻译出版公司.

刘露,刘刚凤,2007.元认知理论在口译教学中的应用[J].成都纺织高等专科学校学报,24(1):32-34.

刘念黎,2006.元认知理论在提高英语听力理解能力中的应用[J].西安外国语大学学报(2):48-50.

刘银燕,张珊珊,2009.英语专业本科口译教学结业测试设计与评估方法探索[J].外语研究(3):74-78.

罗国林,1986.翻译单位及其在实践中的运用[J].中国翻译(3):54-56.

吕俊,1992.谈语段作为翻译单位[J].山东外语教学(2):32-35.

穆雷,雷润宁,1998.试论口译笔记训练中的理解与记忆[J].外语教学(3):82-84.

齐熠,都立澜,李晓莉,2018.试论中医术语翻译中的翻译单位问题[J].术语与翻译(5):37-41.

欧阳倩华,2015.口译质量评估:功能语言学新途径[M].北京:世界图书出版公司.

秦洪武,王克非,2007.对应语料库在翻译教学中的应用:理论依据和实施原则[J].中国翻译(5):49-52.

司显柱,1999.论语篇为翻译的基本单位[J].中国翻译(2):14-17.

司显柱,2007.功能语言学与翻译研究:翻译质量评估模式建构[M].北京:北京大学出版社.

汤君,2001.再探翻译单位[J].山东外语教学(3):18-23.

唐芳,李德超,2013.口译学能测试及其研究[J].西安外国语大学学报(6):103-107.

陶友兰,2010.基于语料库的翻译专业口译教程建设[J].外语界(4):2-8.

王斌华,古煜奎,2014.英汉同声传译的变量考察:基于对同一场电视直播的三位职业译员同传的观察研究[J].中国翻译(6):19-23.

王斌华,2007."口译能力"评估和"译员能力"评估[J].外语界(3):44-50.

王斌华,2012.从口译能力到译员能力:专业口译教学理念的拓展[J].外语与外语教学(6):75-78.

王建华,郭薇,2015.口译笔记认知与非英语专业学生交传质量的相关性[J].外语与外语教学,283(4):68-74.

王建华,2015.元认知理论与交传口译的实证研究[J].中国翻译(3):13-18.

王文宇,周丹丹,2014.口译笔记内容与口译产出关系的实证研究[J].解放军外国语学院学报(2):115-121.

王湘玲,胡珍铭,邹玉屏,2013.认知心理因素对口译策略的影响:职业译员与学生译员交替传译之实证研究[J].外国语,36(1):73-81.

王晓露,2014.口译工作压力及其对策[J].中国科技翻译,27(2):20-23.

吴建平,2006.文化语义学理论建构探索[D].厦门:厦门大学.

邢星,2015.口译学能与口译学能测试的研究[J].外语测试与教学(3):9-15.

徐翰,2013.交替传译信息处理中的认知负荷及其应对策略[J].南昌大学学报(人文社会科学版),44(6):152-157.

杨承淑,2005.口译教学研究:理论与实践[M].北京:中国对外翻译出版公司.

叶舒白,2015.口译错误之辨认与分类[J].[2016-06-12].https://www.researchgate.net/publication/282388258_kouyicuowuzhibianrenyufenlei_-_yeshubai?enrichId=rgreq-1a536aa6-1d1c-4add-ae7b-fe70ef8ff2fb&enrichSource=Y292ZXJQYWdlOzI4MjM4ODI1ODtBUzoyODAzMjYxNDExNjk2NzVAMTQ0Mzg0NjM2ODcxNw%3D%3D&el=1_x_2.

张凌,2006.省略对同声传译质量的影响[J].中国翻译(3):10-15.

张培欣,2017.翻译教学中的汉译英笔译能力测试分项评分量表研究[M].厦门:厦门大学出版社.

张其帆,2002.初探口译员非母语腔调对使用者质量评估的影响[G]//蔡小红.口译研究新探:新方法、新观点、新倾向.香港:开益出版社:400-406.

张威,2015.中国口译学习者语料库的口译策略标注:方法与意义[J].外国语,38(5):63-73.

郑冰寒,谭慧敏,2007.英译汉过程中翻译单位的实证研究[J].外语教学与研究,39(2):145-154.

仲伟合,王斌华,2012.口译研究方法论[M].北京:外语教学与研究出版社.